A
Comforted
Heart

Love is what Matters Most

Kelly Grosklags

Kelly Grosklags

A Comforted Heart

Copyright 2017 by Kelly Grosklags
Published by CWK Publishers
http://www.cwkonline.net

ISBN-13: 978-1979859998
Second Edition

Disclaimer: In the pages that follow, you'll read the stories of patients who have experienced grief and loss. The names have been changed to protect their privacy.

Cover and mandala design: Analisa Kertes
Editing: June Gossler Anderson
Layout and design: Todd Anderson
Back cover photo: Carly G Photography

Printed in USA

Foreword

Words to Give the Soul Repose and Ignite Hope
At the Darkest of Times

A Comforted Heart speaks of the possibility of living a life of hope and peace regardless of life's circumstances, and perhaps this is why the messages contained in Kelly's book have such universal appeal. The beautiful and comforting stories within speak of finding the freedom that comes with forgiveness, living a life of gratitude, being courageous, honoring your feelings and paying attention to your life.

Kelly is an intuitive practitioner and esteemed counselor with deep reserves that allow her to witness suffering and loss in her patients and offer insights that bring possibility and comfort. Kelly's passion to work with the severely ill and grief-stricken commands a soul who is gentle and compassionate and one who can be fierce in advocacy work to assist others to find peace and meaning at the end of life. Working in hospice and having an oncology-based psychotherapy practice over the past 25 years has honed Kelly's clinical skills. She embodies that rare combination of imparting information while weaving in a deep sense of empathy, wisdom and compassion with her patients.

Both compelling and transforming, *A Comforted Heart* was born out of Kelly's strong desire to share the wisdom she has accumulated along the way working with the critically ill and those experiencing loss. Kelly often says that the truest teachers in her life have been her patients. She draws on the lessons imparted to empower others to act with grace and courage as they enter into and move through treacherous and unfamiliar terrain. She has shared her own knowledge and wisdom, as well as that of others, in the beautiful entries within *A Comforted Heart.* The blueprint for Kelly's deep belief that healing is always possible in life even if the cure is not is well laid out in this reflective book.

May the light within these pages give you solace and illuminate hope when needed most.

Barbara Fleetham

Dedication

I am incredibly grateful to the people I have had the honor to care for over the last twenty-five years. *A Comforted Heart* is dedicated to all of my beautiful patients who trust me every day. I have a deep sense of gratitude for my work with you. You have taught me how to live with more intention, purpose, hope and courage. Thank you.

A Comforted Heart

Table of Contents

A Comforted Heart

Preface

This book has been in the works for many years and has finally come to fruition. These writings have been inspired by my own trauma of witnessing the heart attack of my thirty-three year old mother, Sandy, on a grocery store floor when I was eleven years old. Little did I know the influence this would have on my life and my beloved patients' lives. Although my mother did not die from cancer, it was her death that was the impetus for my career in grief and loss, specifically with oncology patients and their families. Through my own grief I continue to learn the lessons that I believe are meant to be shared. Thank you for letting me share them with you.

If you are reading this, you or someone you love has likely experienced a loss of some kind, or been diagnosed with cancer or another illness. You are keenly aware of the daily encounters with the unknown as you experience extreme fatigue, fear and feelings of hopelessness. Yet, you explore spiritual meaning and find the strength to go on.

It is the strong who allow their vulnerability to be known, who find the strength to face loved ones if their news isn't good. Despite people being in the grip of trauma and fear, I witness daily healing in many of their situations.

As you enter into this book, which contains the insights and wisdom I've garnered over the last twenty-five years from the people I have worked with, I hope you will let into your soul the healings that come from their stories. There is no losing or winning with illness or grief, rather integration of all that loss and illness can bring. Much healing and many miracles take place in my work, even at the end of life. I wish for you to receive the wisdom, clarity, hope and support that is intended through the sharing of the narratives within.

Adorations

This is the last entry I wrote for *A Comforted Heart*. For some reason, it was difficult yet, in many ways, the easiest section to create. I want to start with thanking my oncology colleagues all over the nation, especially those in Minnesota. It is a privilege to work alongside you as we enter people's lives in the most vulnerable of times. I learn a great deal from you and admire you all as clinicians.

Through my many years as a board member for Angel Foundation, I have learned the art of giving and the importance of community. I am incredibly grateful to **Margie Sborov** and **Dr. Mark Sborov** for believing in me and always supporting my professional endeavors.

Because of the daily lessons I learn from my patients, this book was made possible. Thank you specifically to those of you who wanted to be included in these chapters through your writings and sharing of your stories. You are the true teachers.

Although there is just one author listed for this book, it has been a team effort and I have an amazing team. Without the time and organization of **Marge Barry** this book would not be complete. Thank you Marge for your time, talent and love

Members of the *Conversations with Kelly* team have consistently believed in me, despite my own wavering confidence. My heartfelt thank you to **Jenny Johnson, Bob**

A Comforted Heart

Sorg and **Connie Sullivan** for being more than team members, but incredible friends as well. You listened, cheered me on, and told me more than once, "You can do this!" I love you.

Thank you to **Chris Henz, Allan Lindgren** and **Jeff Velch** for being a part of the *Conversations With Kelly* team. Your willingness to help with all the shows has freed up my energy to write this book.

I am grateful to my long-time friends, **Tim Beekmann, Patrick Durkin, Cory Ecklund, Jeremy Keippela,** and **Stephen Sporer** for weekly checking in and sharing your love.

Although my friends **Melisa Gesick** and **Cris Eide** do not live near me, I feel they are close. They support me and show me love in whatever I do. Thank you!

A special shout out to **Susan Langston** and **Nancy Lindgren** for being my weekly support group and spiritual guides. You helped comfort my heart every week.

I am deeply grateful to both **Victoria Maghrak** and **Jeffrey Cloninger** for your willingness to read an entry at anytime. You consistently offered genuine love, support and encouragement no matter the time of day or night. I am deeply humbled by your willingness to help and I love you both deeply.

I have many friends who, with deep love and affirmation, have constantly asked about the progression of this book and some who have fueled the project with their continuous texts of excitement. Alas, I wish I could list you all by name, but please know the significance of your endorsements and friendship.

I have the best family in the world. They have gotten me to this place and are the constant foundation on which I land. Several stepped in to help when my mother died. However, I am most grateful to **Susie** and **Jared Greupner,** along with **Sherry Gaertner** for never leaving my side. I will forever be thankful for your constant love that continues to this day.

Mike Gaertner, Earl and Sue Grosklags, Jen, Steve, Olivia and **Joseph Koski,** thank you for all the love, pride and support you show with each professional endeavor. To my family in Arizona and extended family, you have all taught me lessons that help me help others.

My deepest gratitude to my sweet little family who every day remind me what matters most and define what love is for me. **Jeff, Chris** and **Carly,** thank you for your amazing patience when I wasn't always present in order to have time to write. I could not be more proud to be your wife and mother. You inspire me without even knowing so. Specifically, to you Jeff, thank you for encouraging me always and empowering me to be my best self. I love you deeply.

I have an official and extraordinary team that agreed to help with the completion of this book. Have you ever asked yourself "What have I gotten myself into?" It would have been another decade before this was completed if **June Gossler Anderson, Todd Anderson,** and **Analisa Kertes** had not stepped in to diligently dedicate their time, talent, creativity, and support. You are my angels. Thank you for helping create a beautiful resource for those who are searching for healing.

And to my dearest, **Barbara Fleetham,** what can I say to you that will sufficiently express my love, adoration and appreciation for all you have done for the completion of this symbolic book? No one believed more than you that this book would actually happen someday. You have been by my side each and every step for the three years it has taken to birth this book. We have gone through at least ten different titles, focuses and intentions, however, we have landed exactly where we were meant to land. My heart is grateful, happy, proud and comforted because of your unending love and encouragement. Thank you for removing all the obstacles I created so that I could keep the momentum flowing. I hope you are proud and feel a deep sense of accomplishment for a project that we once only dreamed would happen. We did it! I love you.

And finally, to my mother, **Sandy Tremonte.** Through your legacy it is my hope that many will heal and feel their wounded hearts become comforted. I believe you have watched over the entire process of this book and gently influenced it when you could. Barbara and I would often say, "Sandy!" when things fell into place. I hope it honors you, Mom, and that all who read it will believe things will be okay somehow, someway. Thank you for the large role you played in the formation of this book. We don't always understand why loss or illness has to happen, but often, we come to a place where we realize it became the most influential event of our lives. Here's to you mom.

From the Author About the Book

I want to express my gratitude for all who are reading *A Comforted Heart.* This book is deeply personal and has been a true labor of love. The intention in the book's format is that it may be picked up at any time and be a source for what you need at the moment. You do not have to start at the beginning and read to the end. This is a metaphor for me. Life and certainly the healing process are not in a distinct order that you can just follow along. You are able to pick up this book and open to whatever page interests and calls to you. I appreciate many who will read this are limited in energy. I tried to create a book that can be useful despite one having limited stamina. There is an index in the back for your quick reference on what is needed.

On the cover of *A Comforted Heart* there are a variety of pathways that lead to the same place. I liken this to our healing from illness and loss. We don't all take the same path but may end up together anyway. Our paths in life are sacred and at times are meant to be walked alone and at other times meant to be shared. As the designs meet in the middle it reminds me of the work I do daily with my patients. All have a unique path but move toward the center for a common goal, working and moving through their suffering. In turn, I try to meet them there, at their center and mine.

My intention is that the words within resonate deeply and that you will find a sense of affirmation of where you are and discover the messages of hope you need most at the time. I believe some of these messages are so important that I share them in a variety of ways throughout this book. Life is also like this. We don't always experience something just once. We may need our lessons shown to us in multiple ways to gain the wisdom and insights needed for healing.

I have had many profound moments in my life and in my practice, but one theme constantly emerges and that is the power of love. I believe love is the antidote for much of life's suffering. Open yourself to the lessons in the following stories even if the circumstances are not exactly like yours. In the most important ways we are similar and experience the joys and sorrows of being human. May you find the love I have tried to share within and I wish you peace and healing on your life's journey.

Kelly

A Comforted Heart

FIND WHAT GIVES YOUR LIFE
THE MOST MEANING AND PUT
ALL OF YOUR ENERGY AND
LOVE THERE.
KELLY GROSKLAGS

Chapter One
Finding Meaning in Life

Opportunities to Heal Despite Disappointments

So often I work with people who are in situations that may not have the outcome they had hoped for. These situations may include diseases that cannot be cured or relationships that cannot be saved despite our best efforts. There are several people I work with in my practice who obviously want a *cure* for their disease. I, too, wish this for all my patients. Even when cure isn't possible, healing can still happen. I witness happy and content lives from people that work hard to live in the now and focus on the beauty in front of them. I know many living with metastatic and/or chronic diseases who are incredibly content people. I believe this is due to their ability to focus on what matters most, forgive, ask for forgiveness, surrender, trust, express gratitude, find beauty in the simple, appreciate love, redefine hope and keep perspective. All can certainly help heal a troubled soul. To surrender, let go and trust is sometimes all we can do and it is exactly what we must do.

Today if you are struggling with wanting an outcome that may not be possible, I encourage you to release and trust as best as you can; to ask a trusted person to listen to your worries, to find gratitude in what does exist, and still find things to be hopeful for each day. Doing this will allow for more of your energy to be dedicated to those people and moments in your life that bring you joy. It's possible that when we focus so much on a future outcome, we miss the beauty and healing going on in the now.

Perspective

Perspective is everything. I am amazed at how some people who have issue after issue remain grateful and hopeful. I hear a lot of them say, "It could always be worse." I love how perspective can be a healing tool as you keep in mind where you have been, where you are now and where things could go. Allow yourself to find the crack of light in your darkest days. There is a saying, "Crisis translates to opportunity." This isn't to say we can't have empathy for our difficult situations. That is a must. I just find that when I can keep things in perspective I cope better.

Each Day We Are Alive We Can Find Purpose

Each day that we are alive, we can find purpose. Each moment that we are here, we are connected by love to those who matter most. This love, in and of itself, has purpose. Some of the most alive people I know are those living with a terminal disease. Measure life by its meaning. Look for all the ways to heal in your life, even when you won't be cured. We all have a purpose, even beyond death. It is then that our purpose becomes our legacy. I wish you the courage to live, hope and heal. I wish you the ability to be open and find purpose and meaning every day of your life.

A Comforted Heart

Power and Ability to Change

So many in our world feel helpless, frozen in fear, angry, and uncertain. People have said to me, "I wish I could do something to bring change, but I feel powerless."We as individuals are very powerful. We have the ability to change many things, causing a positive ripple effect that spreads throughout the world. Today, do unexpected acts of kindness. Send light into the world, pray for peace, help an elderly person, calm a child's fear, hug someone longer, express gratitude and respect *all* people. If each person did this today, imagine the change in our headlines. Peace unto this world, starting with you.

Stay Connected. Stay Present.

Sometimes I'm at a loss for words. That happened with Sarah, a young woman who had leukemia. She stared at me and asked, "Why won't I live longer? I want longer!" The fear and desperation in her voice is something I will never forget.

There are questions that have no acceptable answers and trying to answer them would diminish the moment anyway. Often what we can do is be present for people. We offer many things by our presence. In this situation, my staying connected offered more than any answer could. What I did say was this, "I have no answer to your question. I want longer for you as well. What I can assure you of is that you will not be alone in this next phase of your illness. I will be here for you." It's amazing what comfort a few words of honesty and love can bring to another human. Stay connected. Stay present. We cannot make the

21

illness or loss go away, but our support can diminish a person's anguish.

Wanting More Time

So often in my practice I hear people talk about wanting more time. They want more so they can witness a certain milestone event, enjoy friends, family and create more lasting memories. These are tender wishes. Their families, in turn, want the same. Everyone seems to naturally want more time.

How are you using your precious time? Hopefully you are doing things you love and spending it with people who matter most. Quality time is very precious. Time that is full of comfort, health, purpose and loving people is such a gift! Be grateful for time with the simple things that make you happy. I have witnessed it often, when people have limited time they notice and appreciate more.

This Is No Longer Your Story

Too often we get stuck in a "story" that keeps hurting us. We torment ourselves by holding onto shame, or pain that does not serve us any longer. I often say to my patients when they continue to ruminate over things no longer in their control, or things that bring up painful memories, "That is no longer your story." It's important for us to feel the big feelings we have over our pains and shames. Feel them and work through them, and let there be room for the healing and release. We control what we hold onto. Today, bless your story and let the narrative change just a bit to be gentle. Love yourself and be more aware of what you allow in to create the story you tell yourself. Your life will have more meaning and purpose after you let go and practice forgiveness and surrender.

Top Three Things That Matter the Most

I had the privilege to work with a terminally ill man in his thirties dying from cancer. Tim was a vibrant man. We started to write a care plan for the end of his life. I asked him, "What are the three things that matter most to you?" Tim answered, "Number one is family; two, my friends; and three, my spiritual beliefs." As we talked further in detail about his end-of-life plan Tim revealed that those weren't always the three things that had mattered most in his life. Too often it was things that stroked his ego, looks, material possessions and money. Although Tim had an abundance of all of them, they often brought on feelings of loneliness.

There is nothing wrong with liking nice things. It's just matter of determining where you put your energy. If you have just a short time to live would you rather be surrounded by those things or people? Which will create meaning at the end of your life? It's good for us to stop sometimes and write out the top three things that matter most to us. This is an exercise that takes great honesty and self-examination. The dying teach us how to live. What means the most to you? How are you living out each day?

Unexpected Gifts

One of the most treasured parts of my work involves hearing the stories of how people receive signs that they are not alone, despite sometimes feeling they are. I had the privilege of knowing Sam for five years. He came to see me to help him deal with the death of his wife and a cancer diagnosis. Sam unfortunately learned about four years into our work together that his cancer had recurred. An hour after Sam had learned of this recurrence, he was in a parking lot feeling fear and worry. As he looked down he saw a rosary lying on the pavement. Sam picked it up and knew he was going to be okay. "I'm not Catholic," he said, "but I feel so blessed by this gift. Spirituality comes in many forms. It is what brings us comfort and provides us with needed support. "The rosary brought him a great sense of comfort and love. It helped him through the difficult times ahead, making things more tolerable. He could feel hope once he became more open to receiving.

About a year after Sam found the rosary he came into my office and said, "I want you to have this as a gift." I was touched deeply by the sweetness of his gesture, knowing what the rosary meant to him. He wanted me to always remember him and the power of believing in something. Sam must have known that he was going to die soon after this exchange. I sure miss him and will cherish the message of this gift always.

By his example, Sam shared other gifts with me. "Express love now. Show your love and gratitude while you can." Also, "The power of believing is medicine." This amazing man has died, but prior to dying, the gift of love and hope helped him live and love well. To love and be loved, it's all that matters. Thank you, my friend, for this gift. You will always be remembered. Your teachings of believing will be shared with many. You lived longer and better with your disease than expected. This likely has to do with the fact that you felt loved and supported. Thank you Sam for your lessons; I will cherish them always.

Things We Learn

There are clichés out there I do not subscribe to, such as "Cancer is a gift," "At least they are in a better place," and so on. What I do know through my own healing and the journey of the hundreds of people I have worked with over the years is pain and trauma *do* take us to a different place in life. We do learn many things through our losses and disappointments. We learn who our people are. We learn about both our own and our support system's resiliency. We learn perspective; it quickly becomes clear what matters and what does not. So, through our pain we can evolve into becoming a deeper person.

Many of my patients find they love life more after these difficult times and become more grateful for their life. It is valuable wisdom to fully appreciate living. Tragedies are not gifts in and of themselves, but these times bring with them lessons that can lead to deep healing and give meaning to our lives. They make us become who we are supposed to become. If you are in the thick of it now this may be difficult to believe. This is understandable. All you can do is trust you will be okay regardless, and that even with disappointment, there is always room for healing and wisdom.

A Comforted Heart

We Need Reliable People in Hard Times

It can be confusing at best when the people in our lives abandon us when we need them most. When we are going through difficult times, we need people for the duration. "Call me if you need anything," "I'm here, no matter when you need me," "We will get through this," and so on are common support phrases that often lack follow through.

Why is this so? There can be many reasons. People who love us do not want to see us in pain, they get too busy, they feel insecure in their ability to help, or their fear overtakes them. Whatever the reasons, the reality is we need reliable people when we are going through hard times. We don't have the energy to invest in people who are leaving us. Our energies need to go into healing.

Make sure you are not so focused on who is leaving that you overlook who is coming. Things get revealed to us that we need to pay attention to. The important thing is to allow people in who appear to have pure intentions of helping. People often speak of the unexpected "gifts" that come from difficult times as well. There are many if we are open to seeing them and none finer than those who come through for us when we need them most.

What Can You Say or Do for Those Who Are Ill?

I am often asked, "What can I do or say to those I love who are ill?" Most importantly, whatever you verbally promise to this person, make sure you're willing to follow it up with action. The hardest thing to bear for those who are ill is people who don't follow through. This creates feelings of abandonment and disappointment.

Try to avoid statements like, "Call me if you need anything." An ill person or their caregivers do not have the energy to be reaching out and calling people. You have to call them for they often believe they are a burden when they reach out for help.

Some things that I think are helpful to say to people include telling them that you care for them deeply; they are not alone; and you're willing to help them in any way that you can and that they will allow. Again, when you say these things, please make sure you follow through with action.

When it comes to "doing" for people you might give them two options and ask them if they would be okay with this. For example, "While you're in treatment we would like to bring dinner every Tuesday night," or "Each Thursday when we go to the grocery store we will stop by your house first to pick up your list," or "Would you be okay if each Friday evening I came over around seven for an hour to sit with you or take you outside?" These are simple offers with profound outcomes.

Hope is the medicine that keeps our spirit healthy. There is no hope that is too small. A dose of hopeful thoughts each day is good for our health.

Kelly Grosklags

Chapter Two
Hope Is Medicine

Does It Take Courage to Hope?

I was interviewed for a national publication regarding hope and living with cancer. I thought the interview could be difficult as there can be a love/hate relationship with the word "hope." I was asked, "Does it take courage to hope?" The short answer is "yes." In my practice I see people daily who dance with hope. It is a bittersweet word to many and most fear they will be let down hard if they allow themselves to believe in something. I see skepticism and fear of hoping act as a protection of sorts. Unfortunately, fear is a major barrier to living and truly being present. Hope has its own life cycle; it is always available. When one is diagnosed with cancer the hope is for a cure. Of course! This is not always possible for some. Then what? Is there no hope? While the ultimate cure may be off the table, you can still hope for stability, tolerable treatment options, NED (No Evidence of Disease), emotional support and love. I work with many people who have said they feel they are on a ride that they did not choose to get on. They often feel defeated that the original treatment was unsuccessful or they have to switch treatment due to side effects. For some this causes significant anxiety and grief. It is important to talk out loud about this disappointment and fear. People will eventually transition to what their next goal or wish is. Anxiety can decrease after the next plan is established.

A Comforted Heart

A beautiful example of this is a patient I worked with who was very optimistic about an upcoming scan and felt the tumors would likely be gone, or at least significantly smaller. He would often say, "I have the choice to be optimistic and hope for the best, or worry and focus on negative. The outcome will be the outcome, but getting to the outcome will be more comfortable if my energy is used hoping for the best." When he got the results of his scan he called to tell me the news was not good; there were more tumors. He said, "Too many to count, but there is still hope. We will switch treatments and my hope will be that it is tolerable and can shrink the tumors. Thank you for reminding me this is a game changer, not game ender."

I do not believe that hope is about flowers, balloons and magical unicorns. Hope is a form of medicine. It allows our minds to have some breaks from negativity and fear. It helps us stay in the moment and believe in ourselves and those who love us. I want people to look at hope like an intention. State what you want. I often hear, "I am not sure if my hope is realistic." I think we need to get out of our heads and allow ourselves to have a full mind-body-spirit experience with the moments in life, including illness. All of us have been disappointed in life and can become bitter, cynical and numb to the possibility that anything will get better for us. This is ultimately our choice. I am a firm believer in feeling and processing our feelings. This allows us the opportunity to release them and make room for new possibilities that help our spirit feel supported and lighter.

A Comforted Heart

No Hope Is Too Small

Waiting can be excruciating. My oncology patients are forced to wait for scan, lab and treatment results. During this waiting it is not unusual for hope to escalate and diminish many times in a short time frame. Again, the diminishing has to do with fear, which ultimately is a form of protection. "I don't want to be too hopeful and end up disappointed." I think what helps many patients is to realize that if the original hope doesn't work, there will be another plan. Hoping does not equate to being intelligent or astute. Rather it is a choice of what energy we want to carry around. Hope is an intention. State it. Let it be your mantra, your prayer, and your anchor for getting through your day.

One of the most profound examples of hope was displayed by a patient of mine who was dying. She was hopeful that the treatment would work for her rare cancer and she would have more time. She and others would say that it did work in that she lived five more years than originally predicted. At the end, she was told that her cancer had become more aggressive and her life was now limited. She told me most of her friends were surprised she was not devastated and they were worried that she was not facing reality. She explained to them, "On the contrary, I am very aware that death is close, but I remain hopeful that my days will be meaningful and that we can show our love and forgiveness, if needed. I am hopeful I will have great pain control and that my appetite returns somewhat now that I am free from chemo. I hope to again taste and enjoy my favorite foods. I hope that my family and friends will realize they are everything to me and that they have been the reason I could do these past five years.

I am grateful for the time I have had and want the time that remains to be the best possible." This is a poignant example of how powerful hope can be. We talked about the cycle of hope and how her original desires have changed but not diminished since her diagnosis. Again, hope is medicine, and its intensity does not need to waiver based on circumstances. She, like many, had strong hope at the end just as in the beginning, but for different things. Each day, write down what you hope for. Nothing is too small. Some examples I have seen are "I hope to be hungry today," "I hope to make my grandson's band concert," "I hope the scan will reveal some shrinkage," "I hope the medicine will ease the pain today." We then repeat aloud this intention of ours throughout our day. Hope is a choice. If your stated hope is not realized, feel, process, and talk about this and hope for something different. I remember the wise words of a patient, "The outcome will be the outcome regardless. I want to feel comfortable in the meantime."

When hope is realized, express gratitude and share with others. I see many pleasant surprises in my field. The dance really is made up of disappointment and delight. Just remember that delight is a possibility as well. Throughout your cancer experience, I wish you the courage to hope and the strength to keep believing in something, as there is always room for hope of some kind.

A Comforted Heart

Choose Hope and Possibility

Daily experiences at my office include seeing many opportunities and possibilities for the light to enter darkness. We have choices each day: how we choose to view our life, where our energy goes, and where we direct our hope. Choose hope, if only for a minute. Our perception is everything. Sometimes, all we can do is just hope to be hopeful someday. Hope is a beautiful break from the fear and worry that can accompany illness or loss. To all those feeling the darkness today, I wish you moments of light.

Sharing Unexpected Surprises

Some wonderful things have happened during my twenty-five years of practice. One surprise was when a young woman who, four years ago, was told that she had just six months to live, recently became a mother. Another gratifying surprise was witnessing the connecting and healing of a family that had been estranged for over twenty years. I've seen medical surprises when a ten percent chance of a treatment working for cancer turns into one hundred percent. And, perhaps the most comforting was when a person who was so scared of dying said, "I wish I hadn't worried so much about this time. It's actually quite serene and I feel more love than ever."

What do all these stories have in common? Each one of them during times of chaos and uncertainty were comforted by the fact that regardless of outcomes, they would be supported and loved.

A Comforted Heart

Fear is powerful and not always accurate. Hidden behind the darkness of fear can be pleasant surprises of comfort, resiliency and hope. If we have support, we can do whatever is in front of us. Step aside fear, you are not welcomed.

Wishing you all the chance to experience any pleasant discoveries hidden behind your fear. Hidden there is hope, love, acceptance, peace and resolve.

Hope Changes

"I have nothing to hope for anymore, I'm dying," Henry told me near the end of his life. I was able to explain to him how hope changes but never ends. Some of the most hopeful moments I've seen are in the last hours of a person's life. Henry no longer hoped for a cure but by the end of our conversation he agreed that his hope for comfort and meaningful connections with the people he loves is still very much alive.

I will often encourage my patients to write down the hope that they have for the day; then throughout the day remind themselves of that hope, even saying it out loud, and in the evening, reflect back on that stated hope. Very often my patients are surprised to learn that that their hope, or a variation of it, was realized.

Hope is medicine. Hope changes. Hope can heal many wounds. Let it be part of your living, your dying and your prayer. If you feel hopeless right now, work on hoping that someday you will feel hopeful. It's a good place to start.

Believing and Hoping

Hope is something we are privileged to feel. Not everyone has access to it when they need it. It takes a courageous person to allow themselves to be hopeful. When you state your hopes, you are letting the universe know your intentions.

Sometimes, we have to shift our hopes from ideal to realistic, huge to small. That's okay. There is *always* something to hope for. I see hope ebb and flow, change and evolve. Even at the bedside of my dying patients, they speak of hope. It's beautiful.

OF ALL THE GIFTS WE CAN GIVE IN THIS LIFE, LOVE IS THE MOST PROFOUND. "I LOVE YOU" ARE THREE OF THE MOST POWERFUL WORDS SPOKEN.

KELLY GROSKLAGS

Chapter Three
The Power of Love

When to Hold on and When to Let Go

"We often are let down by the most trusted people and loved by the most unexpected ones. Some make us cry for things that we haven't done, while others ignore our faults and just see our smile. Some leave us when we need them the most, while some stay with us even when we ask them to leave. The world is a mixture of people. We just need to know which hand to shake and which hand to hold. After all, that's life, learning to hold on and learning to let go."

~Unknown

How Will We Be Remembered?

I have had many conversations with people about their fear of being forgotten once they have died. People living with terminal illness are often excellent teachers on how to better live our lives. I see them as living with more intention, gratitude and letting go of what doesn't matter anymore. When my patients talk about the fear of being forgotten, I ask them to reflect on how they are living now. Are there apologies that need to be given? Is there forgiveness that needs to happen to free up their spirit? Are they being kind? Are they sharing love and taking the time for the relationships that matter most to them?

A Comforted Heart

It is the brightest lights in this world that continue to beautifully impact us years after they have gone. I have asked myself, "What do I want to be remembered for?" My answers then guide me on how to live my best life each day.

Many of my patients who are terminal have said they don't want to be remembered for things that they've owned in this life. They would rather be remembered for the energy and effort they have put into their family and friends, as well as into the world to make it a better place. One person said to me, "Things used to be the way I filled my soul, now it is spending time with my loved ones." We are meant to enjoy the beautiful things that life offers, as long as there is balance with our intimate relationships.

Longevity

In my office, next to my chair, I have a rock that is inscribed with the word "longevity." It was given to me by a beautiful woman named Chris. People often comment on it. Several years ago I sat with Tricia, a young woman nearing the end of her life. As she looked at the rock, she said, "Oh I wish I were going to have longevity. My body is ready to go, but my heart wants to stay." How true this is for many facing death, especially at such a young age. I asked Tricia to hold the rock for a while and think about how she wants to be remembered by those she loves deeply. As we spoke I assured her that another way we can achieve longevity is through our legacy. We live on through generations, memories, pictures of us and the way we lived our lives.

A Comforted Heart

Live a life now that you will be proud of for generations to come. How do you want to be described? How you live now and how you make people feel are both essential to how you will be thought of later. "Loved, gentle, present, funny, loving and giving," were her words.

Legacy: Cards and Letters

One of the profound things I do with people in my practice is help them to write cards for future weddings, graduations, births etc, to their children, partners, parents and loved ones for after they die. When some people realize that death is near they may panic, since they believe they have unfinished business that needs to be addressed. It is most important to my patients that those they love know how much they are loved in turn. These experiences in my office are surreal, yet so beautiful. The lesson in these moments is to tell people we love them, we are proud of them and we want the most for them. We should not wait until the end to make this known.

I was fortunate to be present when a husband received a card his wife wrote for him before she died. It was incredible. He carries it with him daily and, if he ever feels he wasn't enough for her, he reads her card. Love is meant to be shared today. The two things I most often hear from my patients who are terminal: 1) "I want my legacy (memory) to be beautiful," and 2) "I do not want to be forgotten." Our legacy starts now.

It's important, if possible, to have these cards or letters handwritten. Seeing the handwriting of somebody we love helps

A Comforted Heart

keep us connected to them in a meaningful way. This is one way to still be present at those events that will be missed going forward. You do not have to be an eloquent writer or write a novel. It's more about just getting some words of love and meaning onto paper so that you can be represented and remembered in the future.

Being Remembered

I often get opportunities in my work to hold the hand of a terminally ill person. Sometimes I ask people to imagine seeing themselves in the future, participating in their life. What is it they grieve over the most as they realize they will not be physically present?

I remember a beautiful conversation I had with Patricia, a woman in her early forties. Envisioning herself well into the future reading her own children's favorite stories to her grandchildren, she said, "I so wish my grandchildren could know me." I assured her they will certainly know about her. Because of her vision, we arranged for her to record herself reading a favorite book to be played in the future for her grandchildren.

Without a doubt, one of the most important things to us is that we will be remembered, hopefully in the most loving of ways. We need to know we made a difference in this world.

Dying doesn't remove you from the hearts or minds of those you love. Patricia will remain with her family and future grandchildren for generations to come.

A Comforted Heart

Say What Matters to Those You Love

Nobody wants to be forgotten and one of the biggest anticipatory griefs for dying people is to realize the important events they will miss in the lives of those they love after they have died.

I suggest some special occasions to focus on such as birthdays and weddings. One patient I wrote cards with was concerned about what she was going to write. Diane was bed-bound and weak so I sat on the edge of her bed to help her. She took thirty minutes to write to her husband, tears rolling down her face as she completed her card. I thought to myself, "She must have written a lot. I'm not sure where she got her energy." When I asked her if she had written everything she wanted to write she cried and said, "I spent so much time on this because it's important that what I wrote will forever resonate." She proudly shared her card, I was surprised to see only one line, "I LOVE YOU BEYOND WORDS."

Diane said the most important thing was for her to convey to her husband how much she loved him. However, she felt words would diminish her intense feelings. We decided where we would hide the card so that someday he would find it.

Six months after Diane's death her husband called me. He had found the legacy letter and was profoundly moved by that one simple sentence, "I love you beyond words." I shared with him the conversation his wife and I had had around the card and her emotions while writing it. He told me how glad he was that they had told each other daily that they loved each other.

He told me he will read this card every day for the rest of his life. One sentence. Profound beyond words.

Say "I Love You"

I'm reminded of what matters the most and how resilient the human spirit is each time I encounter someone who has experienced a loss. I was called by the husband of a patient who died peacefully in her home. As he was telling me stories about her final hours, what brought us both to tears was how, hours before death with the last of her strength, she opened her eyes, smiled at each of her children and said to them, one by one, "I love you."

So often, we spend energy being anxious about what to say and how to say it. A simple "I love you" is more than enough. Imagine hearing those words from someone you love who is hours away from death. Simply beautiful.

To Be Loved

It is an honor to witness the wisdom of someone who is at the end of their life. That became evident again at the bedside of John, a brave, insightful man who said, "Kelly make sure people know that I love them when I am gone. Please remind them when they feel guilty for not doing enough that they did everything by loving me and never leaving me. I finally know it isn't my weight, appearance, or job that made me happy. It is my family, friends and co- workers. They loved me and never left me." To be loved, now that is something you take with you when you leave this earth. What a beautiful reminder this is of what truly matters most.

Forget-Me-Nots Are for Remembering

I received a thank you card from a patient in the mail. This was a special thank you card as she wrote it before she died. In the card was a package of forget-me-nots; seeds for me to scatter and think of her when the flowers bloom.

She is unforgettable because of the way she lived her life with humor, kindness and how she focused on what mattered most: the people in her life. A good reminder for us is to focus on our legacy every day of this life. How do we want to be remembered? Scatter your goodness now along with your love.

Express Love Now to Those Who Matter

I counsel people who are in intense emotional pain because love was not expressed as before their loved one died. Living with regret is a very hard way to live. It can cause unnecessary suffering for those who carry this around.

Now is the time to say "I love you." *Now* is all we have. If you are suffering regret for not having had the chance to say "I love you" one more time, imagine the person's face in your mind's eye while saying the words "I love you." You can also write a note to the deceased, leaving it at the burial space, under or in an urn. Be gentle with yourself. Your loved one would not want you suffering any more than you already are because they are gone.

Say Their Name

I learn so much about how to live and love from my patients. Each person I have ever worked with wants to make sure their legacy is a beautiful one. They don't want to be forgotten. As we mourn those we love, use their name often and tell stories about them. If you know someone experiencing grief, say their loved one's name aloud. This brings great comfort and keeps their legacy bright, loving and alive. None of us wants to be forgotten. Say their name.

Love Is the Answer

I meet with incredible people who are living with varying experiences and emotions from cancer and loss. There are times the pain and suffering are so unbearable that they are not sure they can tolerate life anymore. Human resiliency is something I witness every day as I watch people endure very difficult treatments that affect their mind, body and spirit. I ask, "Where is it you find your ability to smile and be grateful amongst your suffering?" Invariably the response has to do with love.

Love can be found in so many places: support groups, family, friends and our places of faith. Love is such a simple yet profound answer and I tell people to add more love to their daily goals. Open up and let more people into your life. Love may not cure disease but it is the most powerful antidote. Love allows us to heal regardless of the outcome.

A Comforted Heart

My patients teach me to be more grateful, keep each moment in perspective and find glimmers of light even in the darkest of places. I've seen love make the impossible possible. One example, the woman who was fearful she would not make it through her radiation treatments because of profound weakness. Her entire circle stepped up to take her and stayed each night so she did not have to use energy cooking or cleaning. She was incredibly weak and we were all concerned she would not be able to tolerate the treatment. She was embraced and cared for, therefore, able to focus on her treatment plan and did not feel alone. Love seems to be the answer, regardless of the question.

Have the Courage to Be Open, Real and Vulnerable

In times of crisis or difficulty, I will ask my patients who they are letting in on the situation and who are they asking for support. One response I hear too often is, "Not many. I don't want to burden anyone," or "I don't want to look weak or foolish." Many of my patients feel they have used their allotted time with friends or family when it comes to support. You learn who your true people are by who can tolerate both the difficult and the wonderful times with you. I encourage people to be both authentic and vulnerable. When people ask how you are, if you are not doing well be honest with them. Keeping things inside because you assume no one wants to hear it or because you think it will make you look stronger will only increase your suffering. Have the courage to be open, real and vulnerable. This will lead to healing and better emotional health. Find your people, as they are the ones who will encourage you to take risks and be real.

A Comforted Heart

Allow People to Help

There is something powerful about a group of people who show love to an individual. Most often my patients feel uncomfortable when people want to help. It's important to be open to these offers. We live in a culture where we are taught "strong means doing it by yourself." This could not be further from the truth. Strong means knowing when you cannot possibly do it alone. What I encourage people to think about is this: before they needed help did they donate to a charity, volunteer, or help someone in need? So far, 100 percent of the time the answer has been "yes." The universe works best if we let energy ebb and flow back and forth. Allow people to help. Healing takes a village. You and your caregivers deserve the love that is offered.

Be Open to Receiving Help and Guidance

I feel quite fortunate because I get to witness perseverance and courage daily in my work. Every human being has a courageous nature. If you are at a crossroads where you feel uncertain as to whether you can go forward, take a deep breath and say, "May the strength be given to me to face what I have in front of me. I do not need to do this alone, so I will be open to receiving help and guidance." Often, after people say these words, they no longer feel alone. They feel courageous and strong enough to cope.

Strength is a relative thing; sometimes those who allow others to help them are the most courageous and strong. I hope you will let your courage be seen.

A Comforted Heart

Healing Your Wounds

We have all suffered wounds in our life, wounds that still get ripped open from time to time. We feel frustrated that although we have already dealt with the problem it reappears. What helps to heal a wound is genuine love for self and from others. When we allow love to be a balm for our wounds, we feel safe, supported and not alone. It is when we attempt to "do it on our own" that we only develop a temporary fix. Love that is true and shared with positive intent has the power to bring light to darkness, encourage forgiveness and cultivate acceptance. In doing so we allow deep pain to be released.

Love does heal, and sometimes love comes from very unexpected sources. Certain events or issues we cannot change or cure, this is true. However, with genuine, unconditional love, we can definitely heal with time. Through the power of love, healing leads to a more meaningful and centered life.

Caregivers Are Heroes

I was called upon recently to be a caregiver. It quickly became clear to me that even when I was not "on duty" I was always mentally attached. What I learned is that respite is essential. Daily breaks are a must. I'm not speaking of a break where you get thirty minutes to run to the grocery store. This is an actual break where you nap, meditate, do yoga or quietly listen to music. I often hear from my patients about their fear and worry over their primary caregiver. They worry about burnout and being abandoned.

47

A Comforted Heart

Caregivers often feel helpless or inadequate about how to care for someone they love. Caregiving is difficult. It taps into every fiber of our life. At times, we feel drained emotionally, spiritually and physically. We have multiple roles as nurse, chaplain, housekeeper, cook, therapist and maintenance person just to name a few.

I often speak to caregivers about acknowledging what they give every day: their heart. This should not be minimized. Some days it is all we can give, and sometimes it's the most important. So, if you as a caregiver are exhausted and feeling helpless or defeated, remember love and respect is sometimes all you have left to give and it goes very far.

People in a care facility have at least twelve different people caring for them each day, from the nurse, nursing assistant, and the chef of the hospital to the janitor, housekeeping, laundry staff and many more. As I explain to my families, one person cannot do the job of twelve. Not taking a break and becoming exhausted doesn't prove you love them more. When you are not rundown and feeling overwhelmed, you can better enjoy the intimate moments of caregiving. Your loved one will worry less if you are caring for yourself. As a caregiver not only will you be doing good for yourself by taking a break, you will be reassuring your loved one. You cannot pour out energy from a vessel that holds nothing. Remember to refill daily. Love to all you heroes who are diligent caregivers. Wishing you well.

A Comforted Heart

Listening Is a Gift

I hear from many patients about the struggles they are having with those who are unwilling to hear them talk about difficult things. Many people living with illness need to have somebody they can talk to about emotional issues, including dying. Unfortunately, the response is often, "Don't say that. You are fine, "It's not time to talk about this," or "You have to think positively and not negatively." I feel compassion for the people who love somebody who is ill as I understand they may feel helpless and scared. However, they often need be more open to listening to what is being said and not so quick to shut down because of their own discomfort. Sharing our fears isn't thinking negatively, rather it's a good way of coping with illness.

If you love someone who is ill, have the courage to listen to what needs to be said. People want to be heard, understood and supported. This will help diminish their fears and likely open the door to further discussions and deeper understanding. These conversations have the potential to create more meaningful relationships as well.

If you are a caregiver or a support person, I know you want what's best for the person you love. The things that weigh heavy on the mind will burden the body and create discord with how they feel. Even difficult conversations can lead to beautiful moments. It's okay if you don't know how to respond. Our job is to listen and give our loved one space to discuss. When we say, "If you need me, let me know," I ask that we also let this be about hearing that person's deepest fears and not just performing tasks for them. Take into account that "needs" can be also about desiring a real conversation with someone who won't judge. There is so much that people carry on their minds and in their hearts every day. When shared, it's more tolerable. See this time as a way to deepen your relationship.

What Can You Do for Someone Who Is Hurting?

So often people are at a loss for what to do for someone they love who is hurting. I also see hurting people themselves unsure of what they need for support. Start with the basics. Human touch and connection go a long way. When we hug one another, we connect with their heart. Connected hearts are more healthy and happy, which make for more manageable situations. Hug longer.

Intimacy

Often in my sessions we discuss the loss of sex due to illness or grief. With both, we can experience a decrease in sexual desire or function. This can be a huge loss. I see relationships struggle because of this. If this is happening in your relationship, it's important to remember that this isn't intentional and quite common. It warrants a conversation with your partner rather than spending energy of feeling ashamed.

Intimacy is not the same as physical sex. Intimacy is what lasts longer and has a greater impact on our relationships. Work daily on hand holding, back and foot rubs, lovely walks, intimate conversations, and traveling together. These are lifetime memories that deepen relationships. There is a lot of love within intimacy. Connection has many forms: physical, emotional and spiritual. The most impactful thing is that you are connecting with each other each day.

Broken hearts heal by
being touched by another
person through support
and love. Wounds heal
with time, but the scar is
permanent and represents
the deep bond of love
forever.

Kelly Grosklags

Chapter Four
Grief Is a Bruise on the Heart

Grief Doesn't Come with a Manual

Grief doesn't come with an owner's manual. What we know is that grief has an intensity in the beginning that feels unbearable. Some people spend much energy avoiding this pain as it hurts so deeply. As time passes the work is to find that sacred space in our life that we can dedicate to our grief. We want to embrace rather than erase these painful moments.

If you are newly grieving (1-14 months), it is important to realize this pain will lessen with the right amount of work, support and time. It may be difficult to believe this. However, I speak from the thousands of people I have worked with and my own grief experience. Once grief decreases in intensity there will come a time for most people when they want to stay connected to the grief for it helps maintain a bond with their deceased loved one. The heart will always remember this loss. The scar on the heart is a symbol of the wound. Although you will always miss them, you will learn to live again and, in so doing, will honor the sacred space that will remain in your heart forever.

Every day I see people transforming their pain into wisdom. Be ever gentle with yourself and know that it takes courage, strength, vulnerability and trust to heal from this pain. Healing

53

doesn't mean the grief is over, rather you are becoming less scared of the emotions and likely more comfortable dealing with grief as it arises. We want to reach a place where instead of running from grief we are able to embrace it. I wish you enough time and deep trust that it will someday be okay. Grief in some capacity is forever; deep pain is not.

Grief Is a Narrative of Our Love

I'm periodically called by well-intended medical providers regarding their concern for patients that can't "get over" their grief, even after a year. I remind them grief isn't something we get over. We can and do get through it, but not over it. Someday, as time passes, and the acute phase of grief has settled, you come to realize you don't want to lose the connection as grief can be a connector.

Grief is a narrative of our love for the one who has died. For me, grief hasn't happened in stages, rather I liken it to chapters containing stories of sadness, despair, hurt, regret and even hope and wonder. No longer should grief be shamed for its intensity or duration. All of our sorrows deserve a story. You are the author and can heal through storytelling.

Grief Is the Price We Pay for Loving

Life is about taking risks. Love is risky yes, because there will be a day the physical relationship will somehow end. Take comfort in knowing that love doesn't end. Grief is the price we pay for loving. A dear price, but worth it. Take risks to love. True friendships, family and intimate partners are the riches of our world. Your love will be your forever bond, and as you move through the loss, you will realize this same love that has caused you to hurt so badly will ultimately be that which heals.

A Sacred Space

Grieving people often speak of the "hole in their heart" after a loss occurs. This hole feels like it will always gape open and bleed. At first this hole is like a gunshot wound, causing intense pain, discomfort, fear and even threatening our lives. People sometimes try to fill this space with unhealthy things to numb the pain, such as alcohol, drugs, overeating or overspending.

Over time the wound vacillates between healing and breaking open again and again. Eventually, this hole will become a sacred space within us that is dedicated to only that which is lost.

I encourage you today to be in touch with that space. What memories do you want to live there to honor those you love? No one or anything can completely fill this void; this is a space that deserves to remain open, tended to with love and comfort. Your bond will always live in that space of sacredness. Let your heart stay open and flowing with love and connection.

Grief Is Like a Bruise On The Heart

Grief is like a bruise on the heart and each subsequent loss lands on that same bruise making it tender again. Bruises show us there has been an injury. Grief is like an injury to our soul. When we have been injured we must do whatever it takes to heal. Unlike a broken bone, grief does not have a one size fits all treatment plan. If there were, it would be written differently each day. As you heal, you learn. And as you learn you heal.

The Paradox of Grief

Grief is a paradoxical experience. No one expects that the happiest of times also has the potential to trigger great sadness within. Grief cannot be predicted. It doesn't work that way. Simply put, "it comes when it comes" and can blindside and confuse us when it rears its head unbidden. Joyous celebrations, weddings, graduations or the birth of a grandchild can give rise to feelings of great sorrow on behalf of those who are missing the milestones in our lives.

Rather than subdue, fight or dismiss our feelings during these times of conflicted emotions, the best use of our energy is just to feel them and not judge them. Judging our emotions snaps us back into a place where we look intact, act intact, yet feel disintegrated and inauthentic. As human beings our capacity to feel it all is quite profound. Great happiness and great sorrow can exist simultaneously.

When celebrating the rites of passage in your life allow for the twinges or waves of grief that come on suddenly. Allowing the grief in is one way to honor the continued bond to the person who has died. As it often does later on in the grief experience, the sadness we've allowed in and embraced shifts to a state of gratitude and love. I want to foster this state and feel the joy and sadness of remembering the people I've lost. I feel their presence palpably and in doing so make them a beautiful part of the pivotal event taking place.

Grief Has Many Different Masks

I am often asked about the characteristics and time line of grief, but grief has many masks and looks different on everyone. Each person reacts in their own individual way. For example, some people may cry freely, some may not. This does not mean one hurts less than the other. Culture, age and gender impact the way grief is felt and expressed. In the same family, community and circle of friends, each person will respond and experience their grief differently. Grief can be a crushing and overwhelming emotion so a protective response for many is to try and run from their grief. But grief cannot be bypassed. It waits for us and unexamined grief will often catch us unaware and rear its head at the most unexpected times.

We are encouraged as a society to deal with our grief quickly, pick up the pieces and move on with our lives. However, as we love deeply, we will grieve equally deeply, and naturally, we cannot just "grieve" and put it nicely away. Grief is not something we "get over." Rather, we learn to endure the changes the pain and loss hold in our lives.

Grief does not adhere to a linear time line. Unlike an event that has a beginning, middle, and end, grief is our individual response to an event. Therefore, if you are struggling with how long this grief has lasted go back to how much you loved, then you will realize your grief aligns. Grief is not meant to be judged. It is meant to be felt and transformed in ways that will help give more meaning to your life and bring comfort to your days. Instead of trying to control or predict the experience, surrender is key to letting our feelings be what they are in the moment. We must simply "let them happen" and honor our individual responses.

Eventually grief does lessen in intensity and becomes more of a bond to who and what has been lost. As time passes, we will treasure this connection and allow our deepest feelings to surface. This is where the healing transformation of grief takes place.

Honoring the Lessons Grief Teaches Us

Many of us have experienced moments in our lives that are pivotal, yet we are unaware of how profound until later. Over thirty-five years ago, I experienced "my moment." As I watched strangers perform CPR on my mother, I didn't realize how impactful that moment would be on the rest of my life. Grief is a lifelong process. It ebbs and flows. I have learned this is the good news. Years later, I now realize the "it" (death) that traumatized my life for many years is now what transforms it.

With time grief does lessen in its intensity and we can learn from it. Today I honor all the lessons in this grief, even the painful ones, and invite it to sit with me as I, the student, am ready. I'm grateful for the time and healing in my life. I also wish you time, learning, patience and healing as you grieve.

A Comforted Heart

A Place for Grief

I often visit my mother's grave. It is when I am there that I feel a true sense of connection as I am not distracted by the outside world. I allow myself to "feel" the feelings and I am not concerned with much else but reminiscing and paying attention to whatever presents. I will often sit back and observe all the ways grief and love are being expressed by visitors throughout the cemetery. I am a big proponent of having a place to visit, sit and focus our grief.

I am a strong believer that this designated place connects us with our deceased loved ones and helps in our healing because we are forced to be present. It doesn't necessarily have to be a cemetery. I suggest a special place such as a park, a tree, a rock, a sacred space in the home, etc. The purpose is to have somewhere that we can become quiet and focused in our grief.

For example, I've worked with people who have spread the ashes of a loved one in another country, but have dedicated a bench at a park here at home in memory of their loved one. I've also worked with people whose loved ones are buried in other states or countries and I recommend, for example, they plant a remembrance tree in their yard. They can visit these places on special occasions or when they want time to reflect in quiet. Some say, "I can grieve anywhere." This is absolutely true and we do.

I wish you all the comfort of a sacred space to feel and express whatever you need throughout your lifetime. Grief is meant to be honored as it is the continuing expression of love. Be with your grief in that space that holds the memory of your beloved. These moments can be precious for those who need time to focus their grief.

Happy Mother's Day to All Women
Who Nurture and Those Who Grieve

Mother's Day can be a 'trigger day' as many posts are up on social media sites. They can be difficult to read if your heart hurts. Each year my daughter and I garden on Mother's Day. While planting, I admired the bleeding hearts. Their very name symbolizes both beauty and pain for those of us who have lost their mother. Today, I grieve that my mother never met my children. However, celebrate their grandmother, nana, and aunties who love them so. This is the both/and component of grief.

For those experiencing grief on this day, allow time for the pain. Create some designated time to be alone and light a candle in memory of the one you are missing. Ask for their love and strength. Despite the grief it is okay to also celebrate the important women in your life and the children whom you have influence on. Bittersweet are those days that give us permission to be intentional in our grief as well as joyful. Please honor whatever you feel today. Happy Mother's Day to all women who nurture, and peace to those who grieve. My heart beats sadness and joy. Both make up the collective of a grateful heart.

Father's Day Grief

Father's Day can be a day of grieving for many. On this day you may be missing your husband, father, grandfather, or some other important male figure in your life. I've learned that special days, like Father's Day can conjure up difficult emotions and I've worked with many who feel conflicted because of this day. People may be deeply grieving for a deceased or estranged father. All too often people try to fit into an "either/or" way of living. Either I'm sad or I'm not. Honor all that you are feeling, both joy and sadness.

If you are a father grieving a lost child, a letter to your child on this day may feel cathartic. If your father is deceased, it may be helpful to purchase a Father's Day card, write in it and leave it where he is buried, or in a special place that reminds you of your dad. You can also write a message to your father on a rock and throw it into a body of water after meditating over it. There are many ways to connect in grief. How isn't as important, as the intention of doing.

For those who struggle with this day, I wish you the courage to feel it all and then the peace and love of those in your life.

Child Loss

Throughout my years as a therapist I have often heard from the bereaved about the sadness they feel when people avoid mentioning their deceased loved one's name in conversation. This tends to be especially true for those parents who have lost a child. Parental bereavement can be one of the most difficult grief journeys a human can experience. It is not part of the natural order to lose our children before our own death. Parents will tell me that they feel they have lost their entire past, present and future because their child died.

If you know someone who has lost a child, please refer to this child by name. It is important to bereaved parents that their child never be forgotten. I assure you, you cannot make a parent sad by mentioning their child or acknowledging their pain and suffering. They are sad because of the death, not because of your concern. We honor those who have died when we speak of them, especially by name.

If you are grieving the loss of a child, my deepest and most heartfelt condolences to you. It is my hope that you will often hear your child's name spoken and therefore, honored.

Losing a Pet

Grieving over a sick or deceased pet is a very difficult and real grief. You will not likely experience the unconditional love anywhere else in your life like you have received from your pets. For some people, pet loss is even more traumatizing than human loss.

For those of us who have owned a pet, we know the uniqueness of this bond. It's unconditional and always forgiving. Pets do not judge us and they take great joy in the simplest of things. It has been said we could learn many things from our animal friends. The grief after a pet dies is as unique as the bond was. We lose our constant. We lose the connection of non-judgment and full acceptance. Pets appreciate us even when we are not at our best.

After a pet dies, expect to feel deep sadness for a while, especially when coming home and the greeting committee isn't there. I encourage ritual when a beloved animal dies, whether it involves family reminiscing, lighting a candle, or burying their pet's favorite toy. Let this ritual have a purpose in acknowledging the loss.

Loving a pet is a privilege, and the love they give in return is truly a gift. Never minimize these feelings by saying, "Oh I'm being silly this was just a pet." No, again this was your constant, accepting, forgiving, and unconditional friend. Many humans do not love with this purity and remember that because of you, your pet has lived an amazing life.

Grief During the Holidays: New Rituals

Holidays can be difficult for many. Grief, loneliness, illness, financial issues may all be troubling you now. I work with people who are anticipating that the upcoming holiday could be their last. They are pressuring themselves to feel joyous and make it their best one yet. The same is true of my patients who are deeply grieving. They are trying hard to make this season joyful, when in fact, it isn't for them.

Too often we focus on the wrong things. It isn't about the material gifts, the cards we send or the perfect dessert. It is about the conversations, the reminiscing, the affirming of love. During the holidays, wherever you are in your life's work, surround yourself with those you feel most comfortable with. Even in your deep pain, let love be the *present* and let it *be* present.

During the first year after a loss and going forward, I encourage the following ritual: While sitting with friends and family in a circle, each person takes a turn going around, looking to the person to their right, and telling them something they love about them. Let love penetrate your holidays, even when they feel dark. Love can carry us. It comes from many sources.

Three Wick Candle

Here is a beautiful ritual for anyone that is missing a loved one this holiday season. Purchase a three-wick candle and place it in the center of the table. The wicks represent the past, the present and the future.

Light the first wick, representing the past, and say this blessing: "To honor the memories we share and your legacy, we ask for strength as we remember you."

Light the second wick, representing the present, and say this blessing: "We ask for comfort and healing as we miss you. Please give us strength as we live now without your presence."

Light the third wick, representing the future, and say this blessing: "To honor the connection and love we will always share, we ask for the strength to face the unknown without you."

A Comforted Heart

As the wicks burn, each person around the table can share a memory about their loved one. The flame is a universal sign of light. May lightness enter the darkness of your grief.

Saying Goodbye

I sit across from people every day who are suffering from a "goodbye" of some kind. We know that those who have to say goodbye abruptly are more prone to a complicated bereavement. As difficult as it is to watch our loved ones linger with illness, it is a gift to have this time to express love, reminisce, express gratitude, say goodbye, ask for forgiveness and apologize if needed.

If you are grieving a sudden loss, it is important that you be ever gentle with yourself. It is especially important that you not put grief on a time line as the first year is learning to work with the numbness of shock and disbelief. The second year can almost be more difficult as the reality has presented itself with a vengeance.

Saying goodbye in any circumstance has its difficulties. We become so aware of our vulnerabilities as we face a different life without our beloved. What I have learned in my own life and through the countless stories I have heard on the front lines with the bereaved is that grief is more manageable without regret. Regret is one of the darkest places in grief. It also hijacks our healing and forward movement. How do we minimize regret? We live life *now* in the most loving way we can. We express our

65

love, we forgive, we apologize, we accept, we let go and we show up for people.

Yes, there is a part of grief that often involves regret. But I know that if all the aforementioned actions are practiced in life, regret can be minimal. If you can say that your loved one was loved and felt love, then you can release regret. Regret is a futile, ugly energy in grief and keeps us stuck. I encourage all of us to live our lives, starting now, expressing our love, gratitude, remorse and vulnerabilities. Someday, we all have to say goodbye to those we love. Goodbyes are never easy. Make them meaningful.

The Highs and Lows of Grief

So often I hear, "What a ride this is!" "This" refers to the reactions people have in relation to a difficult life experience. This reaction to something or someone we have lost is called "grief." In our initial grief we experience many conflicting thoughts and feelings. People often ask me if I think they are going crazy because one minute they feel okay and centered, and the next minute they feel like their world is coming undone. For the rest of our lives we will experience feelings around this loss. This actually is more common than not. As time passes so will the extremes of the highs and lows of our grief.

Like the waves of the ocean our waves of emotions will peak and subside. You will find that there will always be an energy of movement within your ocean of grief. However, time allows for more calming waves than those that come crashing down in your moments of initial grief. Even years after a loss you may have moments when you feel like your waves are crashing over you once again and you are drowning as a result of something triggering your grief. Try hard to surf the wave, reassuring yourself that it will always subside and you will be let off into calmer waters. With time you may even be able to see some beauty within that ocean of grief.

I wish you peace as you navigate your waves. Remember, your spirituality, family, friends, pets, and anything else that supports you, will be on the shore where you can come back and find comfort. You are never alone.

Grief Is a Lifelong Reaction to a Loss

Please remember grief is not an event that starts and stops; it is a lifelong reaction to a loss. Grief is the last act of love we can give to those we cared for during their lifetime. Where there is deep grief, there is great love. Grief will not end entirely, rather it will ebb and flow. Know that it won't always feel as intense as it did early on. It's a passage, not a place to stay. Grief is not a sign of weakness or a flaw in one's character.

Grief is the price we pay for experiencing deep love. It is a privilege to love, therefore a privilege to grieve. Your bond will always be strong through your memories. So today if you are not allowing yourself to feel your grief, you are depriving yourself of the continued connection and bond to a true love. May love, comfort and the courage to feel accompany you on your healing path.

A Comforted Heart

Our Hearts Do Not Forget

Working with individuals who are grieving the death of someone they love is one of my greatest professional privileges. I get to witness human courage and persistence every day. These are painful yet sacred moments.

I encourage all those I see for bereavement work to have goals for the day and keep expectations minimal during the first six months after the death. We are very limited in our energy and ability to focus, therefore we must keep things as familiar and simple as we can. I often hear people say, "I'm scared there will come a day I won't remember their voice or face." Naturally as time passes, details fade. However, I can assure you that with pictures, videos, shared stories and the memories that remain, your beloved will always be present in your mind and heart. One thing I will do is look at a photograph of the one I miss, then close my eyes and imprint that face on my mind. I've done this many times over the years. If details of the person fade, this is not a reflection of my depth of love for them, rather it's my mind's way of naturally healing.

What *will* always remain in memory is the love and connection you shared. Our hearts do not forget. They store the memory of love forever. If you have recently lost someone, write down some of the details about them that are important to you. We don't think that we will ever forget, however, it is natural as time elapses, our memories are not as precise with the details. Love and connection are forever stored in your heart. Closing your eyes and imagining your beloved while placing your hand over your heart is a beautiful way to reconnect.

Quieter Griefs

I once worked with a person who needed to leave her home of many years to receive more one to one care. It reminded me of the many griefs we often face in our day to day life but do not give much attention. Leaving a home can be a difficult loss. It is important that we and caregivers pay attention and be true to that grief. Sometimes these "quieter griefs" can hurt even more because they are often not acknowledged like the more "obvious" griefs. It will feel more supportive if others acknowledge our pain. However, it must start with us. We must first acknowledge and allow the grief we feel.

What are the quieter griefs of your days? Acknowledge them to yourself. Speak of them and let them be heard. This helps to validate them. Grief is not always measured in the way society wants us to define it. If we are feeling a reaction to a change or loss, then we are entitled to grieve.

If we felt attached to someone or something and we lose it, we will have sadness and possibly experience other emotions as well. To not have this loss be acknowledged by others is difficult, but to not acknowledge it ourselves is tragic. Allow yourself to feel what you feel without self-judgment. Authentic sharing about it can be helpful. Find your trusted support system. I hear people say things such as, "I know this is foolish to feel this sad. It's not like someone died." This statement diminishes feelings. Only we know how attached we were to what has been lost. Please don't silence your pain by not acknowledging it. Quiet grief is meant to be heard as well.

Embracing Change After the Loss

Families I work with after losing a loved one are trying to deal with their devastating loss. I admire the mantra of one of these families. "It's all about being comfortable with things being different. And trusting 'different' isn't stronger than us." These are profound words for any change we encounter. Things will never be the same after a loss or a diagnosis of a life-changing illness. Embracing the change rather than fighting it will allow for more energy to deal with the pain. I encourage you to acknowledge, feel, fall, get back up, hope for better, love again and survive one more day. That is grief.

Grief Is Always Present in Our Lives

Grief is always present in our lives, whether anticipated, acute, or lifelong. As time passes our grief changes form. It makes our life more real. Our perspectives change. Big things seem smaller. Stress from before the loss can feel insignificant now. We often discover a resiliency within us we never knew we had.

We can't hide the pain, nor do we want to. I want to express assurance to all of you acutely suffering: it will get more tolerable. Until it does, let yourself have your big feelings. Allow others into your pain and remember, it takes a brave person to be vulnerable.

A Comforted Heart

Grief is a lifetime experience. It can make us more authentic, wiser and spiritually more open as we do our healing. You are forever bonded to what or who has been lost as you allow the presence of grief in your life. Don't chase it away, rather *be* with it, and find what it needs in order to be comforted. Hugs, prayers, nature, music and love are all beautiful tonics. I wish you the ability to find your center in your grief and *be* at peace.

Grief Becomes a Welcome Companion

I have learned that grief *eventually* becomes a welcomed companion because it is what remains of the bond we had while physically together. If you are in the acute phases of your grief, you can only just be with it now, surviving each moment, breathing deeply. As time passes, the sharpness will likely lessen. After years of surviving a traumatic loss I have found a place for my grief. I welcome the opportunities at times to just cry, laugh and ponder in quiet about all the memories. They don't cut like a sharp knife any longer. When will this happen you may ask? It will happen when it happens. All in due time. It's different for everyone. When we can *be* with the pain, it diminishes. When we *run* from it, it picks up momentum and catches us. Grief has much to teach. Hopefully you will come to a time where you look at your grief and say, "It's okay to stay." Until you are there keep breathing deeply. Let the pain sit and gently tend to it with help from your support system.

A Comforted Heart

Experiencing Many Feelings at Once

In grief we have the capacity to experience many feelings at one time. Sometimes it confuses people how they can feel such sadness and still find something funny. When we love big, we create a large heart space that can hold all that we feel. It is best to not feel guilty or judge what you are feeling. These emotions only keep us distracted from our healing work. Look at it this way: When we are in relationships, we feel it all. So the grief related to that relationship will mirror what our connection was like before the death. Let go of any expectations of the way you "should" grieve and be at peace with what you are feeling and how you are honoring your grief. You will grieve in whatever way you need to as long as you are not hurting yourself or others.

Grief Is Humbling

Just when you think, "I've done this work. I'm doing okay," a trigger comes up and then the grief jumps up like a jack-in-the-box. The best we can do is to feel what has risen. Acknowledge rather than judge. Ask yourself this: "Is what I'm feeling okay?" The answer is likely, "yes" and this answer allows for no judgment. Be humbled by grief; this makes the process more authentic. Grief needs tender love in order to heal. You will likely feel more comfortable with whatever feelings arise after having more time with grief.

A Comforted Heart

Loneliness of Grief

Loneliness is a painful feeling experienced by most of us at some time in our lives and it is a very common emotion in grief. This is not the same as being alone. Have you ever felt lonely in a room full of people? When people talk to me about loneliness, it has to do with the feeling of not belonging, of being left out or being different. Grief will magnify this. Whatever it is that we lose, we are hyper-aware of others who have what we have lost. What is important is to have self-compassion instead of self-pity.

I often encourage people to write down what they are grieving and then what they wish to be different in their lives. Be vulnerable and tell someone about your loneliness. When you share your vulnerabilities you have the opportunity to be heard and feel more connected. We only need one person in our life who is present with us and who loves us. Too often people focus on having many friends; one is sufficient for now. I understand some things just can't be changed; however, it's important to connect to someone who loves you. Being heard can remedy our feelings of being lonely.

Listening to the Voice Within

All too often I hear in my sessions the judgments placed upon the bereaved by people who make statements such as, "You aren't grieving enough," or "You are grieving too much," and "Are you still sad?"

A Comforted Heart

Although many people are well intended, these statements are not helpful; in fact they are hurtful. Grieving people are doing enough self-judging, often critiquing whether they are grieving in the way "they should." Grief is unique. It comes with its own intensity and time line for each person. Sometimes it's not denial we see, but rather a choice to not let grief in because we can't handle it at that particular time. We honor the pain; we realize it's there, but for now we do not have the capacity to deal with it. Rather than denying grief, we are practicing good self-care.

Each of us has an intuition of what we need. Some of us are more fluent in understanding what our intuition is telling us than others who need more time to pay attention and learn. When we are quiet enough we can hear the most within.

We Experience Grief in Our Own Way

"Kelly, will it always be so hard? It's been fourteen months and I still feel so raw." This was a question asked of me by someone who lost her best friend of twenty years. I often get asked questions related to when will the pain end.

We all experience grief in our own way. Even when we are grieving the same person within a family we all react in our own ways. To me grief is like sitting on the shore of the ocean when at certain moments the waves of grief come up and wash over you and you get drenched in your emotions. At other times you are sitting, aware of the ocean, but instead of being washed over by a wave of despair you are enjoying the setting sun and feeling joy. It's important to not live in fear or run from the

74

waves, rather let the emotions wash over you, feel and integrate them. It is then that you can continue on.

Grief changes over our lifetime. We won't always be in the acute phase of pain, but if we don't accept those moments when waves of despair wash over us, we will instead experience a more complicated and prolonged period of acute anguish.

We Will Forever Be Changed

"Kelly, when will I feel myself again?" "When will this grief be over?" These are two questions I hear variations of quite often. Very likely the answers will be difficult to hear. When we have a significant loss in our world we will forever be changed. We will no longer see the world through the same lens. To strive to get back to exactly where we were before the loss is an exercise in futility. Working to "get over" grief is an impossible task. Where then can we best put our energy for healing? I have found that it is important to honor the feelings that arise.

Many people have heard me speak of grief as our bond to what or who is lost. It allows us to feel many feelings: sadness, anger, fear, confusion, and even joy. These feelings help us remember many things about our beloved and keep us present in our healing. In the beginning of our loss (the first two years) we feel unbearable pain at times. These years are spent going from surreal to real in regards to the loss. From "Did this really happen?" to "This really happened."

We eventually move through this acute pain and it settles. However, through time you will have "grief intensities" where the feelings arise, sometimes without warning. These are the times we must let it wash over us, feel it, talk about it, pray, meditate and learn. It passes.

May your pain become softer and may you embrace the different person you become after a loss. People survive loss every day. It takes a village to heal. Let others in and the pain shared will be more tolerable. I have come to be grateful for the opportunities to feel my grief . These experiences have allowed me the chance to meet many beautiful people along the way and discover deep wells of resiliency.

Two Things in Life That Are Eternal

There is not a statute of limitations on our emotions. It should be expected that if the person you lost was someone you were deeply connected to, then your life will be forever impacted by the void. Our well-intended friends and family do not want us to be hurting, so we feel their well-meaning pressure to "wrap it up." There is no such thing in grief. Love and grief tend to be the two things in life that are eternal. You cannot have one without the other.

If you are concerned your grief may be unhealthy or if you are depressed, schedule an appointment with a healthcare professional. Grief is a continuation of our connection but now it has taken a new form. We can grieve and still have a meaningful life. Grief should be an ever-moving experience. It can take on an unhealthy form if we do not let grief flow when it arises. When we self- judge, we cog the flow. When the flow stops, we can become physically, emotionally and spiritually ill. Grief is made up of many parts: sadness, anger, beauty, fear, joy, confusion and love.

It's Not a Relapse

Mark was in his mid-twenties when his wife died of a rare cancer. Fifteen months after her death, he came into my office and said, "I was doing so well. Now I have had a relapse in my pain. I had thought it was over." Mark sounded defeated and shameful. His family had been positively reaffirming and reassuring him that he was being "so strong" as he seemed to be coping so well. Now he had had a "relapse."

My response to Mark was that I do not see relapses per se; I see awakenings to the moment where grief appears, and you allow yourself to be with it and honor what it says. Think of the process of healing from grief like reading a continuous book. If you find yourself in more intense moments, you have reached a chapter where there are more triggers. Grief can intensify with smells, songs, dates, seeing a picture, etc. If we can spend energy *with* our feelings, we allow for a gentler movement through the pain. What does it mean to be with our feelings? It means cry if sad, talk about your frustrations when angry, or sit quietly if contemplative. This is not contingent on a time line, rather honoring your feelings when they arise.

The Parts of Us That Still Remain

There are parts of ourselves that remain within, and through healing we meet or rediscover, often for the first time, those parts of us. Every day I hear from people how difficult it is to not feel whole when they are grieving. They often do not recognize themselves, or remember what matters to them any longer. One thing I will do with patients is have them show me pictures of themselves prior to their loss and tell me about who they believe they were at that time. We will then talk about what parts of themselves that still remain. Of course, we change after a loss- that is inevitable. What we need to realize, however, is we are still a person who loves and needs love.

If you are in grief and feel you have lost yourself, ask a trusted person to tell you things that they still see and recognize within you. It can be comforting to recognize parts of yourself that have been forgotten. The essential part of who you are will always remain.

Grief Versus Depression

What is the difference between grief and depression? How can I tell if I am depressed? These common questions can be a fine line indeed. Both grief and depression have similar characteristics and can be debilitating. What I look for to determine the difference is the duration and intensity of "symptoms." It is common to want to be with a loved one after they die, however, an obsession or a plan to make this possible is considered a crisis and the person should be seen immediately in an emergency room or by a mental health professional.

If you or someone you love is experiencing extreme fatigue, hopelessness, insomnia, inability to concentrate, significant weight loss or gain, marked changes in appetite, significant irritability and/or difficulty finding joy in anything for two weeks or more, an evaluation for depression is recommended. Medication does not treat grief, as grief is not an illness. However, if indicated, medication can help balance the brain chemistry so that the grief can be worked on and managed. Grief is very painful and depression exacerbates the pain. Both deserve your time and attention.

Let Grief Flow

I was profoundly impacted when I toured the 911 Memorial and museum in New York City. I was in awe of this tribute as it was so thoughtful and poignant. As a grief therapist I often look for the metaphors in things. I saw many. The grief and sadness were apparent, representing all religions, genders, ages and races.

As happens in grief, each person reacted in their own individual way. I witnessed tears, sighs, smiles, anger, and just staring while they reflected. Onsite there is a waterfall, a wonderful representation of the tears we release when in pain. I wish we could all be this waterfall in our grief: To release, and have a place where our tears are collected as a community stands by and understands our feelings. After all these years the waterfall's tears run daily. This cleanses like we do when we cry.

In grief, honor your individual responses. Surrender is letting our feelings be what they are, not trying to control or predict them. We must simply let them happen. This is where healing and transformation of grief takes place. My hope for all of you experiencing grief is to let it flow, let it be observed and transformed as a community stands by you holding the space of love and healing. We all deserve the permission to grieve.

Love and Grief

Grief is the price we pay for loving someone. I work with many people who face multiple losses and wonder if they will survive or if the pain will overcome them. Where there is deep grief there was once great love. Some may say loving is risky, as we know every relationship ends someday. I like to think of loving as a privilege and that the privilege is worth the risk. It would be a lonely life if we chose to withdraw our love in order to avoid pain later. When we allow grief to be present, we are connecting ourselves to that person that has died. This isn't to suggest we will remain suffering forever. Instead, it is an encouragement to feel the grief when it presents itself.

I have learned that when we acknowledge our feelings, we will feel more connected to those we have lost as we move through the grief. Write about it, speak, scream, cry, or sing. When we allow ourselves to be one with grief, we cannot help but to be present. There is healing in this presence. Think of your grieving process as an opportunity to reconnect through memory.

Studies have shown that health risks occur when we do not express our emotions. Grieving is hard on the immune system. It taxes it even more if we stuff our emotions. I must also add that

A Comforted Heart

grief is not always hardcore sadness or anger. Grief can also be feelings of happiness when memories are shared. Happiness is also meant to be expressed.

We feel to heal. Today, honor what you feel, no matter how long ago the loss occurred. I wish you the courage to feel, grieve and connect. May your memories now serve as a bridge from feeling alone to feeling connected. If you are struggling to access your feelings, lighting a candle with music can help the mind access what your heart is feeling. I wish lightness for your hurting hearts.

A GRATEFUL HEART IS ONE THAT IS FULL OF PERSPECTIVE AND APPRECIATION FOR THE MOST SIMPLE THINGS IN LIFE.
KELLY GROSKLAGS

Chapter Five
The Heart of Gratitude

A Blade of Grass

"I've lived with the uncertainty and fear that a cancer diagnosis can bring for almost twenty years. Currently, I'm living with stage IV breast cancer. People ask me all the time how I manage to live with grace and have a terminal illness at the same time. I don't think there is a magic recipe for how to handle it. I live with it by practicing gratitude, compassion and trying to stay in the present moment. I can do everything possible to fight back the cancer, but ultimately I can't control it or life in general. I can only control my attitude and how I choose to live with cancer. I've learned that fear and gratitude find it difficult to exist in the same space. When fear has knocked me off balance and I've landed in a heap on the ground, I look for the smallest thing I can to be grateful for. As cancer patients we know that some days finding something to be grateful for can seem impossible. So I start small, really small. Maybe it's even being grateful for the blade of green grass in front of my face as I lay in the mud and find gratitude. Search for it, it's always there somewhere and it will bring small amounts of joy back into the darkest of places. Gratitude helps me to regain my balance."

A Comforted Heart

This is a remarkable testimony written by Judy E. about living with cancer and her profound perspective on gratitude.

Focusing on What We Have

These words resonate deeply: "I believe it's time we focus on what we have instead of what we don't have. This makes for a more grateful heart and peaceful spirit. In the end it's not about who broke your heart. It's about who mended it. It's not about the times you put your self-esteem in the hands of others, but instead, the days when you knew your worth. It's not about those who let you down, but rather those who always held you up. It's not about the many people who desired you. It's about the ones that valued you. In the end it's not about all the times you were called beautiful, it's about all the days you felt it."
~Unknown.

"THIS"

A beautiful story about gratitude was told to me by one of my wonderful patients. Kim and her family were hiking on difficult terrain. As they struggled to make it to the top, a family member asked each person, "What will be your reward for doing this difficult hike?" They answered in turn, "a martini," "chocolate," "pork chop." When they got to Kim she said, "THIS." The actual ability to climb was her reward!

It was a profound hike for Kim because she has metastatic cancer which has spread to her bones. Yet she appreciated that her body could still do the climb. What some may view as an ordeal, others see as a privilege. I believe perspective is the root of gratitude. What is your "this"? What is it that you are grateful for that maybe others take for granted? Gratitude has the power to heal and make life more meaningful.

Simplicity and Gratitude

When patients choose to stop treatment, I talk with them about the importance of living out the rest of their life with those who matter most to them. Each person has spoken of their desire to make life simple as they are approaching the end, and what little it takes to bring them joy. It's humbling to see what matters once people let go of all the unrealistic expectations placed on ourselves and others. It comes down to simple and beautiful connections.

Several years ago, I met with a man who told me he only had two to three weeks left to live. As we talked about what he wanted to focus on in his final days and weeks, he brought up things most of us may not notice in our daily lives and take for granted. I now appreciate my hunger, the taste of my food, the comfort of a nice blanket and the smile on a child's face. I am grateful to be reminded of the simple blessings.

Gratitude Is Essential for Happiness.

Illness holds the opportunity to bring people closer. Worlds get smaller and what matters to people becomes more evident.

When presenting at oncology conferences, inevitably, people come up after to share stories. There is something quite beautiful in sharing these moments as people tend to reveal their hearts' deepest concerns. A few years back after I was done speaking, Bill approached me offering to share his story. He, his wife and daughter all have has cancer. One would not expect him to feel much joy in his life. Bill was full of joy as he spoke about the love they share between them. He was grateful for the love and time his family made daily for each other.

What struck me was his continued ability to hope and his authentic gratitude for his family. Bill's feelings were real and as he walked away, I had an insight. Perspective is the key to gratitude and gratitude is essential for happiness.

Notice Now What We Hold

I was recently at the bedside of a young patient who was dying. This wish was her legacy: "Do not wait until the end to appreciate what is now." Let's notice *now* what we hold and let it be enough for today. These are simply beautiful words. Gratitude heals.

Opportunities and Lessons Within the Loss

Difficulties in life are a given for us all. Sometimes we wonder if we will ever "catch a break." As with any tragedy, and/or loss, there are opportunities and lessons within. We become aware of our own resiliency because we were tested. Oftentimes, we learn who our true people are and who we can and cannot count on. These are important learnings. Some of the most joyful people I know are the ones who have had the most difficult lives. With time, we are able to find wisdom and even gratitude amongst our pain. Gratitude transforms us. It can change our story.

A Comforted Heart

Today I am grateful for the power of courage. The courage to grieve, heal and transform.

Being Grateful

It's true, gratitude heals. Some of the most grateful people I know have the least in material value. I'm in awe of people who can appreciate what they have, even when, by society's standards, it doesn't seem like much. For those you are grateful for, tell them. For things you are grateful for, express appreciation. More blessings will find their way to you once you verbally express your gratefulness. A wonderful mantra to remember, "For what I have and who I have, I'm grateful."

Words to Live By

A personal mantra can be used a grounding tool to bring you back to your center at any given time. A mantra is defined as an affirmation or prayer that is repeated as often as necessary to assist you in achieving a sense of calm, inner peace and balance. Mantras can be a place of refuge and helps connect you to your spiritual core when dealing with situations that are overwhelming or when you feel full of dread. Simple mantras such as "all is well", "this too shall pass" or "please help me" remind you to breath, slow down and not panic. When you slow down and look within, you will find what words comfort your soul. When you make them your own you empower yourself. Use them when feeling uncertain or full of despair and you will enter the center of your being and take sanctuary.

A Comforted Heart

Consider the use of a daily gratitude mantra that enriches us with its focus on our being the recipient of many things we take for granted in any given day. Many tell me of rushing through their days feeling disintegrated and disconnected from their lives. When we ruminate about the past or worry about the future we squander the precious day that we are living in the moment. Whereas there are many things in life we cannot control, we do have the power to direct the flow of our energy and how we respond to the ups and downs that is part of being human. When we live a life centered on gratitude, a shift occurs that allows us to release disappointment and enhance our capacity to feel happiness, contentment, and a deep sense of appreciation. Expressing gratitude reminds us to trust our lives purpose and to see that many unexpected blessings happen throughout the day. The more we reflect on this the more we recognize gratitude's amazing power to transform discontentment into a state of wellbeing. Simple expressions are often the best such as "Peace fills my heart", "Thank you," "I am grateful for this day," "I have everything I need today" are beautiful examples of a daily practice cultivating gratitude.

Personal mantras, such as a gratitude mantra, help us hold clear intentions on our healing path and engage our energies to promote a tranquil and fulfilling approach to life. Let the power of a personal mantra assist you in staying grounded in your beautiful story.

A Comforted Heart

Bedtime Gratitude Meditation

Gratitude gives us a joyous appreciation for all the good in our life. Both science and spiritual teachers agree that a gratitude practice leads to an increased sense of happiness, hope for the future, and promotes positive feelings. What we focus on prior to falling asleep has a significant impact on our waking hours as sleep aids deeply in our healing. Focusing on gratitude as we end the day allows our subconscious mind, the gateway to our deepest feelings and beliefs, to be awakened to messages of thankfulness as part of our inner reflection on the meaning of our day. Consider cultivating a bedtime gratitude meditation.

Before falling asleep bring to your awareness someone or something you are grateful for. It can be a person, animal, or experience. Often people choose to reflect on the "big things" in their lives but focusing on something "small" helps us to see that many beautiful and unexpected gifts come our way each day that we often don't see or appreciate such as a beautiful night sky, the delights of a simple meal or an unexpected kindness. Focus on the details of what you have identified and remember the experience, the encounter, the feeling of it and take it in as deeply as you can.

Then say "thank you, thank you, thank you". Repeat this process five times or more. Always include yourself in one of those times. This is how self- love is fostered.

A Comforted Heart

This practice will strengthen with time and you will come to savor the peaceful moments and feelings of grace that come from this simple meditation.

A Comforted Heart

It's how we live now that impacts how we are thought of later. Shine bright while you are here.

Kelly Grosklags

Chapter Six
Living the Now

The Guest House

"This being human is a guest house.
Every morning a new arrival.
A joy, a depression, a meanness,
some momentary awareness comes
as an unexpected visitor.
Welcome and entertain them all!
Even if they are a crowd of sorrows
who violently sweep your house
empty of its furniture,
still, treat each guest honorably.
He may be clearing you out
for some new delight.
The dark thought, the shame, the malice.
Meet them at the door laughing and invite them in.
Be grateful for whatever comes.
because each has been sent
as a guide from beyond."
- Jelaluddin Rumi

A Comforted Heart

"I Am Loved"

There is a big power in the words we say to ourselves and others. Be mindful today of what you are saying to yourself. The things we tell ourselves is what shapes our reality. Today, I encourage us all to use positive affirmations of "I am strong, beautiful, capable, worthy, enough, healthy, lovable, talented, wise, and supported." There is such power in our words, so we must check in frequently to see what we are saying to ourselves. As we each have an inner being, (inner child) a good rule of thumb is to ask yourself, "Would I speak to a child the way I'm speaking to myself?" Gentle, loving words make for happier, healthier people. Today, start with "I am loved" and go from there.

The Gift of Presence

To be present with someone in this lifetime is one of our greatest offerings we can give to another. Very often we are too distracted by the many things in our lives to be completely present with the moment. Whether distracted by electronics, thoughts, people, or addictions, we lose much of life's beautiful moments.

Each day I learn from those who are critically ill. I see through their eyes a newly found appreciation in "simple" moments and the pure beauty of things they admit they didn't notice or appreciate before they became sick. They speak about how the illness has forced them to stop for a while and try hard to just *be* in the moment. When we are with people, at a show, listening to music, or watching the birds, wouldn't it be wonderful if we could quiet the noise and truly *be*? Life is much richer when we are entirely in the moment.

So today let us *notice* more. Let's put away the distractions and truly be with the moment. We miss so much. Slow down. Share the gift of noticing and being present. Enjoy your day and the simple pleasures.

"I Love You" Heals

It is remarkable to me how many people grew up never hearing the words "I love you" spoken to them and how it carries over into their adult lives as they are unable to say those words to others. We all have a love language of how we show our love. I understand speaking it isn't the only way, and I also know the words can be empty if actions do not follow.

As a psychotherapist who specializes in loss, the implications of being neglected this way is a "hot topic" in grief work. People are tormented over the lack of hearing "I love you." Of course, it is something to be said only if you authentically *feel* it. Today is the day to go outside of your comfort zone and say it to those whom you love. This moment is all you have. "I Love you" heals.

Love Is Meant to Be Shared

I had the privilege a few years back to attend a lovely memorial service. The son of the gentleman who died, wrote his father a wonderful two-page letter dated 12/25. In this letter, all the things that matter most were talked about. It was sweet to listen and hear "I love you dad and thank you."

The son said in this letter that he knew this would likely be their final Christmas on earth together, so this was essentially his gift. I cried as I sat and listened. We all want to be remembered as a loving human being. I am mindful that we are creating our legacies each day that we are on this earth.

This letter once again reaffirms the importance of our words; the importance of telling people we love them. The greatest part about this letter was the father had heard every word before he died. All too often, we save our words until it's too late. Love is meant to be shared and expressed now. Now is all we have. Cherish it.

Be Intentional with Your Words

Often during my day I hear countless stories about hurtful words that have been said to my patients. Words have a power like nothing else. I have counseled people about painful words spoken to them twenty years ago. They are unforgettable. When you speak, be intentional with your words. They are forever. They represent you. When you listen, demand respectful words be said to you. "Thank you," "I love you," "I'm here for you" are some good choices to make. If you feel angry towards someone, you can still be mindful with your words. Anger doesn't have to be cruel. Today, let our words only help or heal.

This Moment Never Again

"Live in just this moment." This is not always easy. Grief, shame, and fear can bring us to the past, as well as the future, creating unnecessary suffering. The Buddhists' say, "This moment, never again." If you can create a word or phrase that will bring you back to now, it will be helpful. Practice this many times until it feels natural.

Let yourself experience what you are feeling. If you are caught up in the past, you may experience feelings of depression. If you are trying to figure out the future you may feel anxiety. Breathe and be here, *now*.

I worked with a lovely young woman who was dying. After her death her husband shared a story with me that exemplifies the practice of living in the "now." He spoke of how he tried to avoid being with his wife at the end of her life as it was so painful for him. He had multiple excuses for why he couldn't sit with her. Then something happened and he needed to be with her for caregiving reasons. To his surprise she opened her eyes for the first time in a long while, smiled, and said, "I love you." This beautiful moment would never happen again. He would have missed it had he not been living in the present. Remember, this moment never again.

Letting Go

One of the more difficult conversations I have with people is when the pain created by somebody in their life doesn't match reality. Illusions are painful. People can hold on tightly, even to those that have hurt them. They think it's better and safer to stick with the known, rather than risk the unknown. I know it's painful to think of letting go of something or someone in which you have invested so much time and effort. Please, love yourself enough to let go of that which no longer feeds your soul or possibly never did. We get one chance at this life and we deserve to be authentically loved and respected. So today, have the courage to be real. Have the strength to demand genuine love and respect from all in whom you invest your time. Cleanse from your heart-space those that hurt you. It makes room for those who truly love you.

Difficult Relationships Have Purpose: Learning the Lesson

Many of us experience personal relationships that are not for our highest good, nor encourages our best self. We fight over and over with ourselves to let this person go. We intellectually know what we need to do, however, we are emotionally stuck in the illusions of this relationship. It's human to hope for different. It's important, though, to be quiet enough to hear your intuition, and then listen and believe it. Even difficult relationships have great purpose. They are the teachers of how to let go and show us what we want and deserve.

Those Who Show Up and Those Who Don't

It is common for my patients to talk to me about changes in relationships when they're going through illness or other difficult times. Being abandoned by friends, especially those with whom they have had long-term relationship, is a unique loss that has many deep layers. It's important to honor our feelings of rejection or sadness when people we expect to be there for us do not show up. It's equally as important to notice those that do. It's not about the number of people, it's about the quality. It just takes one person that we can trust and who loves us to champion us on our path of healing. Today, focus your energy and light on those who will walk with you at your darkest times. Release those who cannot. Love does heal and sometimes it comes from the most unexpected sources.

We can only put energy into the people who expand with our stories. Grief certainly can be felt from the realization of those not showing up, and at the same time, joy is felt from the discovery of new love and support. Gratitude is felt for those who can expand with us.

Open Your Hands

One exercise that may help you in letting go is to squeeze your fist tightly as you imagine that what you are struggling with is in that fist. Maybe it's fear, a grudge, worry, or anger. Now, open your hand and imagine laying down what you have held for so long and release it. When all your energy goes into holding onto something so tightly, it's hard to receive love or anything else from anyone because our fists are closed. It's also difficult to receive the desirable things in life. Have the courage to open up, to let it go, to surrender. You will be amazed at what you can receive with open hands.

A Comforted Heart

Losing Control

Not too long ago, as my plane was landing, I thought of how many times I had that uneasy feeling whether we would land safely. Realizing that I had no control over the situation I told myself to breathe and trust the pilot.

So many people, whether suffering deep grief, difficult health situations, relationship or financial issues feel out of control. They speak of "losing control of the wheel" and feel like they are ready to crash at any minute. Much of this anxiety comes from expecting an outcome we believe we need to be okay.

If you are trying to take hold of things not in your control, let yourself surrender and be comforted by those you trust. We look to our medical team, clergy, therapist, and/or loved ones for the needed support. People, somehow, make it through situations that they once believed to be impossible. Trust you will be okay. Even with unexpected or undesired outcomes, people can cope because of love and support. Instead of trying to control a situation, put your energy into comforting yourself. Also, releasing self-blame and worry is essential for your well-being. I wish you the ability to trust enough.

Worry Less

I recently heard a common theme repeated as I was holding a hand at the bedside of a patient who was close to death. I asked him what he would change if he could go back in his life. He answered "I would worry much less." I have asked hundreds of dying people this same question, "What did you worry about that was so important?" The answer is often a derivative of "I have no idea." What precious moments are you being robbed of when your time is spent worrying about things you cannot change?

All of us are guilty of worrying about things that may never happen. Today, try to surrender some of your worries which will help your energy level, and be better for your overall well-being. Treasure the day, the moment and those you love, this can help decrease your worry and create a sense of calm.

Coping with Fear

I see my share of people who are tormented by anxiety and worry on a daily basis. Often I'm working with people who are worried about an upcoming scan result, a biopsy result, a difficult family conversation that needs to be had and/or the changes in our world.

What's important to remember is that being scared is natural in life and we make our situations more difficult when we add catastrophic thoughts to the feelings. Our coping can become compromised. This type of thinking threatens our overall well-being and health. It's important to reassure yourself in the moment and remember that no matter what the results or outcomes are, you will be okay and there will always be a plan. People tend to isolate themselves when they are fearful. I encourage people to share the cause of their worry with someone they trust. You will be amazed at how much better you can cope with things if you do not feel alone.

A Comforted Heart

Fear can be diminished when shared. The "evidence" that we create in our heads is false until proven true. Again, it is important to stay in the moment. Imagine yourself breathing in white peaceful light, and breathing out a dark toxic energy will help keep you grounded. Going for a walk, meditating, talking to a trusted person, and working hard to stay in the moment while breathing are all very good things for coping with fear and worry. Remember, there will always be a plan.

Fear Isolates Us

Years ago, a gentleman I worked with shared with me his profound wisdom. We engaged in a beautiful discussion about life and regrets. He shared freely that he wished fear hadn't stopped him so often from taking risks or chances on love. He had let past hurts keep him from seeking love. He thought he was protecting himself, when actually in the end, he only hurt himself. He spoke about how relationships take effort, and that good ones don't just happen. His words of wisdom, "Learn from past pains. Be smart about it, but don't let the anger or fear keep you from trying again." Fear only isolates us. If he had a do-over, he would have given love another chance. What are you needing to let go of today? What fear keeps you stuck? And what courageous thing will you try?

Dealing with The Unknown

Fear is indeed one of life's biggest obstacles. In my work with those who are ill, there is often an understandable fear of the unknown. This applies to us all in reality. When people get to the point where they can somehow embrace the unknown and surrender control, it diminishes the fear. What I tell my patients about the unknown is this, "What was once your unknown in the past, is now your known. Things you know now were not always as clear or comfortable to you. Every day I see people become more confident and trusting in themselves. This is because unknowns will eventually become familiar and clear *or*, often, what is feared does not become reality. We can trust that when we get to that place that feels unfamiliar and scary, we will be guided to what we need." Choose to spend energy on the now and remind yourself to trust that you will be okay and loved.

Living in An Alien World

The following is a poignant description of being diagnosed with cancer by Cynthia F.

"The minute I got 'the call' I was abducted by aliens who captured me and took me onto their spaceship. I had no reservation for this trip, no itinerary, and no chart from which to navigate. I didn't even know my return date. The aliens were dressed in white lab coats and spoke in a foreign language that I'd never heard before. Within seconds I was thrown into a subculture with absolutely no preparation, whatsoever. Within twenty-four hours I was in a surgeon's office to discuss invasive ductal-something-noma. Flooded with statistics and terminology I had never heard in my life, I remember feeling like I was underwater trying to listen to someone on the surface speaking. They were making sounds but I really couldn't make out any of the words. They all blended together and I couldn't understand any of it. I had entered a world of strange people, with strange tools, and unfamiliar vocabulary. Nothing was as before; the food I was allowed eat, the language I began to speak, and sometimes even the friends I thought I had. Soon enough I looked like an alien myself. There were weeks when I didn't even recognize myself in the mirror. The sound of my voice was the same but my body was not mine. I was immersed in this foreign culture but, as with any foreign culture, it only takes about ninety days before you become nearly fluent in the language and the ways of these strange people. In fact, you grow to like these strangers. You depend on them and develop a routine with them. I suppose this is much like soldiers in war or prisoners in jail. You quickly learn how to navigate your new situation and adapt to the new standards and ways of living.

In the beginning you try to work your cancer treatment into your busy schedule, making time for second opinions and surgery around your work, meetings, and family schedule. Overnight that transforms into carving out time for work, meetings, and family events around chemo and rest. In no time, cancer seems to dictate every minute of your day and you somehow squeeze the rest of your life around this protocol. As soon as you've got the routine nailed down, however, it's over. Chemo is done. The aliens bring you back to earth and push you right out the spaceship door. There is no re-entry guide and no orientation back to 'normal life.' You feel as though you've been in a time warp. You have seen things and done things you can't explain to anyone, yet no one else has changed. Everything is the same. Except you.

A Comforted Heart

Time goes by and you eventually begin to re-assimilate back into your own culture. Your strength improves, you take on more and more things that you had to let go of when you were sick. Soon enough, you are doing things that six months ago you couldn't have done. You have found your 'new normal.' A delicate balance of the best of the 'old you' combined with the best lessons learned from cancer, creates the 'improved you.' It's not an experience I would wish on anyone but I have realized so much about myself on this journey that I may not have otherwise ever learned."

The Waiting Game

All too often my patients have to play the waiting game: Waiting for blood work, waiting for scan results, waiting to see if their body will accept a drug and respond, and so on. If you have ever had to wait for important news, you can relate to the anxiety that builds. The clock feels like it stops and with each passing hour or day you feel less in control than ever while you wait for results that hold power. Many people have to wait to see if a new treatment will work or not. They often hear, "We won't know for awhile. It will take time." We are all called to be patient at times when it seems unbearable. One person said to me, "All I do now is hurry up so I can wait."

I witness daily the power of the mind and how it can play horrible tricks on people, filling our thought space with catastrophic fears and making it difficult to function. I find many of my patients become anxious from waiting because they think they will "lose control" or "go crazy" if it's difficult news.

A Comforted Heart

This isn't true. You won't go crazy. You will be scared, yes, but you won't go crazy. Remind yourself that whatever the news will be, you *will* be able to handle it. Our unknowns become our known quite quickly and as humans, once we know, we can deal with it.

What can we do in these times to help us cope and keep living? The irony is that we are worried about results that may change our quality of life or, even possibly, cut our life short. Yet precious life is passing us by as we worry. We want time to slow down in general, but in these moments of waiting we wish time would speed up. I strongly encourage you to express the fear, worry, and difficult thoughts you are experiencing with someone outside of yourself. You will do best in these times if you reach out to support people, allowing for transparency and vulnerability. Talk openly about what it feels like to wait. Let other people know you are feeling the anxiety. Illness and loss are lonely experiences indeed. However, these feelings of being alone and scared can diminish with the help of others.

I think one of the most important things to remember while waiting is that the outcomes will be what they will be regardless of time spent worrying. Worrying just depletes our energy. There will *always* be a plan to address the results. You will not just be dropped and forgotten. It isn't unheard of that plan B worked better than Plan A. So, reassure yourself with words such as "I will be okay regardless," "I am not alone," "I am safe," "There will be a plan," and "I am always loved." If just for a moment we get relief from worry, it makes the waiting time more manageable.

Waiting and Waiting

Waiting and waiting. It's what so many people with an illness are forced to do. Wait for appointments, wait for results, wait to see if things improve or if they get worse. The waiting can be very difficult. Is there anything you can do to make it easier? Yes, the answer is "distraction." During these times of waiting, find things that distract you. Distract yourself with people, places, or things that make you feel better. Plan something you've never done before. Go to a movie, read a funny book, pray, take a walk, play with children and animals, or learn a new hobby. It's also helpful to do any kind of exercise you can tolerate to get all of that internal energy moving through your body.

Some people will imagine they are putting their concerns into a balloon and releasing it to the sky. Someone once told me, "I release my fears in a balloon to my Guardian Angel (grandma) who can handle the burden better than I. It just feels good to let them go."

Anxiety and panic causes people to think the worst. Stay in the present and remind yourself of the power of thought. Sometimes just saying the word "now" can help you come back to this moment. One practical tip for this time of waiting is to start free-writing in a journal. Begin with, "Right now I'm consumed by these thoughts," and just keep writing. You are the only one who's going to read it, so write freely and from the heart. The purpose is to get these thoughts out of your head and your body and onto paper. Until you have the information you need, your anxieties need a distraction and that's where the writing comes in. What often happens is that people will begin to transform their anxiety through their writing, which can diminish the intensity and bring about a sense of peace.

Times of Waiting Bring Strength and Courage

All of us at one time or another have had to patiently wait for something that will change our lives forever. It is understandable why sometimes we lose patience and feel despair. The waiting often creates fear, vulnerability and ambivalence. This poem by Jeffrey D. Cloninger captures the moments of waiting and shows that often, even when we are being challenged, moments of strength and possibility can exist. Sometimes we need these times of waiting so that our courage and strength can evolve even more.

Every day I walk here I see this tree.
And I think of it and all the other trees it surrounds and shelters.
And I think it's magnificent.
And I think of how far and wide its branches have grown:
Leaf-bare now, but soon to burst open in abundance, again.
And I have faith that we, too, will experience a new season of
growth and fecundity,
All in time, when it's time.
Know that hour is approaching.
And for now, know that inside, to host to all that goodness, the
tree patiently prepares.
It knows no other way.

—Jeffrey D. Cloninger

We Are Not the Disease

It is common for me to hear people who live with serious illnesses to speak of themselves and define themselves as if they are, or have become, the illness itself. It is so important when we speak of ourselves that we remember we are a whole person with likes, dislikes, values, hopes and dreams. One of the best ways of taking control during an illness is to not give in to *becoming* it. The concept of "both/and" applies here very well. We both live and struggle with being sick, and we are people who have lives despite the illness. Each day I recommend writing something about yourself in the morning that has nothing to do with illness. One example may be "I am a person who loves music." Listen that day to music and find yourself getting lost in the words or instrumentals. At the end of the day, re-read this, and go to bed reminded that within you are many attributes. Another example, "I am a loving mother or father." Look at pictures of you with your family, or call them to tell them you love them. At the end of the week, you will have an amazing list and a gentle reminder that your illness may have taken some things from you, but not everything.

The body responds to where our thoughts are directed. Be careful with self-talk if you identify only with being sick and unable. Remember, you are a whole person, you are many things, however, a diagnosis is not one of them. Rather, you live *with* a disease, not you *are* the disease. Some of the most alive people I know are the ones who struggle with many medical issues. I believe it is because they keep in the forefront who and what they love. Living with a disease must be one of life's most exhausting tasks. You may be surprised that you will find energy in the exercise of daily reminders of *all* that you are. It is so easy to forget this when we have to constantly deal with stress.

Emotional Side Effects

A good portion of my days are spent with people living with cancer. I see daily the cruelty of this disease both physically and emotionally. Many of us are accustomed to the side effects from medications. Those dealing with serious illnesses are well versed and spend countless hours weighing the burden versus the benefits of side effects on their quality of life.

Mental and emotional side-effects also occur from living with a serious illness. I counsel many who struggle with depression, anxiety, extreme grief and fear. This is directly related to the daily burdens that potentially threaten their lives.

For so many, the torment of not being able to plan too far into the future is a loss. As well, it is natural for people to make friends with others who live with the same disease as they understand each other in ways most cannot. These relationships also become a source of loss, as death is eventually part of a serious illness. These compounded losses can interfere at times with the ability to focus on living. Emotional side effects must be addressed just as nausea or pain would be. They make living more challenging. I find when people have opportunities to express their fears, they cope better. Feeling supported can help

110

diminish emotional side effects, which are as real as the physical ones.

Depression/Anxiety

Clinical depression and/or anxiety can be difficult diseases to understand. Those living with them have said it is hell to navigate the symptoms and daily effects on life. It's hard on both the person with the illness and those who love them.

Unlike a physical illness, depression often leads people to hide because of embarrassment, stigma or feeling like "this is all in my head." Research shows that people with depression/anxiety will have a better chance of a cure or being healed if they have a good support system. If you love someone with these diseases, stay close to them and involve them as much as you can in the outside world. It can be difficult to love somebody with a mental health issue because they we feel powerless in how to help and often get pushed away. Although the illness itself causes people to isolate, the best thing is to be surrounded by loving and caring people.

It takes great courage to face the day when you have anxiety and/or depression. Everything can be a struggle. Everyone can be a struggle. We need to start realizing as a society that these are both medical conditions that need to be treated. If you were struggling with constant back pain or headaches, you would allow yourself to see a physician and likely ask your loved ones for support. Please do the same if you are depressed and/or anxious. Mental health has better treatment outcomes if a support system is in place. You didn't choose your mental health therefore no blame or shame is needed. However, you can choose your response.

If you are suffering today, let at least one trusted person be with you and support you in getting the help you need and deserve. It's important to remember, depression/anxiety are illnesses that are caused from a chemical imbalance of the brain and need medical attention and tender loving care, the same care a broken bone or a heart condition would need.

Sometimes the Impossible Becomes Possible

If you are struggling to believe that things could get better for you, let me tell you a story. A patient I worked with had a sudden turn in his condition and was admitted to the hospital. Uncertain about what was going on, the family all gathered. The medical team did not offer much hope for improvement and encouraged them to say their goodbyes. He was declining quickly.

Even I was surprised as I had just seen this man the week before and he seemed stable and in good spirits. We all came together to say goodbye. They cried and repeated stories of the love they had felt from him during their lives. It was very touching. I scheduled a family appointment to discuss the stressors of the past weeks. I opened my door and there *he* sat, looking very healthy and glad to be back. When questioned, he spoke of a new treatment option that was apparently working for him, but equally attributed his current recovery to deep spiritual work that he had done with his family.

Sometimes the impossible becomes possible. If you're dealing with illness, grief or other difficulties, it's important to remember that healing occurs on many different levels. I wish you the ability to trust and see healing in many areas of your life.

The time following a difficult decision should be met with gentleness towards self and others. Energy and thought that go into these decisions can exhaust the spirit.

Kelly Grosklags

Chapter Seven
What's Dying Like?

The Difference Between Death and Dying

The difference between "death" and "dying" comes up often in my sessions. "Death" is the moment you take your last breath; "Dying" is the process of getting there. When a woman is having a baby, she writes a birth plan. I also write "dying plans" with my patients when they desire it. This consists of information from the advance directive down to what kind of music they want playing in the room while dying, or who is able to visit.

It's a time to be specific and voice what *you* want, not what you think others want. This is an important time in one's life and should be given much consideration. Communication is key to a good dying process and a good death. In this plan, we aggressively address pain and suffering. People are generally relieved after completing these plans. It's important that you pick one or two people who will make sure that these arrangements can be implemented.

Dying doesn't have to be ugly. It should be a time of peaceful goodbyes, forgiveness, memory sharing, quietness, and even joy. A time to be shared with those you love, and a time you feel nothing but love and safety.

A Comforted Heart

Living and Dying

Many times over the years I have been asked, "What will dying be like?" I can only answer on behalf of the countless people I have been privileged enough to care for at the end of their lives.

We die how we live. In other words, the things and people that bring us comfort in life will be desired in our dying. If you are a person who likes quiet and are more introverted, you will likely be more comforted by a serene, less crowded room. If you are a person that finds great joy and strength in your faith, you will likely be comforted by prayers and readings of faith. It is an unknown time for us all. However, many are comforted to know that there will be people to care for them and to guide them.

I have witnessed hundreds of deaths and I have given birth twice. I see many similarities in the two processes. The most profound one is that we are taking the journey as an individual, but are surrounded by as many people as we need. These people are wanting the best for us in the transition. When discomfort occurs, there is help. When we feel scared, there is support, and when we are ready for the final moment in both birth and death, we are encouraged to let go as it is the natural way of the process. To surrender brings relief from suffering.

Many of my patients over the years have spoken about not so much fearing the final breath, but more the dying process. People acknowledge they feel sadness for what will be missed on earth and what will be felt by those who grieve them. I encourage each person with a life-threatening illness to think about enrolling in palliative care and/or hospice care. Palliative care is a newer concept to many in the United States. It is an important program and approach to managing symptoms and helping people who may still have years to live but need help with the chronic part of illness. Hospice is for those who are terminal and generally have a life expectancy of six months or less. Having worked in both, I am a strong believer that these programs help people *live* well and eventually *die* well. These programs are not about giving up. They are about comfort and support to help the quality of one's life.

I was working once with a wonderful man who was days away from death. As I was holding his hand he turned his head and asked, "Kelly, what is dying like?" I answered, "Just like this." He smiled and said, "I can do this then because I have support and I am comfortable." It was a beautiful moment I will never forget. He demonstrated how to be brave by surrendering and trusting that as symptoms arose for him, we would address them. We have resources available to help ease pain and suffering.

If you are reading this today and have a life-threatening illness, you do not need to go through this alone. If you have fears, give them words. Worrying is understandable and can be diminished if you surround yourself with a good team. Life and death are both more doable if we have people to guide us. So much in this lifetime is more possible when we feel supported.

A Comforted Heart

Living While Dying

I often hear people speak of being apprehensive about falling in love or making any future plans because they're uncertain which path their disease will take them down. I know, as humans, we do our best to avoid anything that may potentially cause us pain.

It must be difficult and exhausting to live life this way. Until you have a definitive prognosis, why not enjoy life now? Furthermore, even with a limiting prognosis, people can continue to enjoy simple beauty in life. I often counsel my patients that one of the best actions against disease can be moments throughout their week where they live their life as if they were disease-free. Yes, I am a believer in being realistic, but in some cases what appears to be outlandish can actually be a possibility. It is risky to allow any disease to define who you are.

I encourage you to incorporate the disease as one piece of your life while trying hard to live as a whole person. Without knowing *when* or even *if* your fear will ever transpire you still have life to experience. In the meantime, live, dream and hope always.

Fall in love, plan a beautiful hike or weekend trip, buy that new furniture and dream about a winter vacation. Not one person I've met has regretted experiencing happiness, even if it was for a short time. I wish you the courage to dream. Remember, we all live until we die. I suspect we all want to fill our lives with meaningful moments up until the end.

A Comforted Heart

Deciding to Stop Treatment

Throughout my career I have seen people struggle with many decisions. Because of my specialty, I spend much of my day discussing treatment options for cancer. I can say that 100 percent of the people I meet with put tremendous thought and energy into their treatment decisions that are made with the healthcare team. In any type of advanced disease or terminal illness, people are on a roller coaster ride regarding choices of whether to continue or stop their protocols. This is scary and exhausting. They often second guess themselves and want some type of guarantee for their decision.

If you are reading this today and are the caregiver or loved one of somebody who has decided to stop treatment, I have genuine empathy for you. I know for some there is a deep sense of relief to have the decision made. The best thing we can do for the people we love is to trust their decisions and realize the amount of effort and energy that went into them. If you are confused about why decisions were made ask for clarification for your loved one or their health care team. Rarely do I see someone who didn't spend hours, weeks, and months researching, deliberating and consulting before making a choice. We must never accuse anyone of "giving up," rather affirm them and support them for honoring the messages their body and spirit are sending. The majority of my patients know when it's time to switch or stop treatment. The thing they need the most is support and understanding from those they love.

A Comforted Heart

Talking with Children

The capacity and resiliency of humans amazes me. The ability of Laura, a young mother, to sit down and look her children in the eyes and tell them the truth, that she is dying, was profound. Laura's bravery resulted from her love for her children. "The medicine has stopped working. Mommy is going to die," she said. True to their age group they asked, "When?" Laura's response was one she and I had created and she delivered it beautifully. "This is not something I know or can choose but as things get closer or change I will tell you. It's important you keep playing and doing all the things you love to do. You do not need to be fearful. You will be included along the way."

We cope better with honest information, and if we feel included (age appropriate) we do better. Kids are not meant to be sheltered from family grief. They are meant to be included as much as they appear to want to be. And if they don't, it is okay. By involving children, we allow them to have more time with the change and loss occurring in the family. Anticipatory grief has purpose, it helps us ease into a loss and prepare for the inevitable. It is a time we can ask for forgiveness, forgive, show gratitude and love. It is a good time for children to ask questions that could make a big difference in how they cope with the loss. The truth (again age appropriate) and inclusion makes all the difference in how children will be long term. If we pay attention, children will show us what they need.

A Comforted Heart

The Power of Loving Words

When working alongside the bed of a dying patient, one of the most rewarding moments is when the family asks me, "What should we do now?" Feeling their high anxiety level, I will show them, rather than tell. I take the patient's hand, look into their eyes, or stroke their brow and say simply "You are safe, loved, and I am here." As in life, in dying, we do not want to be alone. Simple words, simple actions with profound implications. Oh, the power of loving words!

Be Present with The Dying

If you have a loved one who is dying, you may not know how to "be there" for them, and you may even wonder if you are capable of the tasks at hand. First, I know people do the best they can. I also know that too many people doubt themselves, which depletes their energy for caregiving.

Over the years many people have asked me what they can do for their loved ones who are dying. They feel helpless, scared, and inadequate. A person who is dying requires people to be present with them, to reassure them they are okay and that you, their loved one, are going to give them support and do whatever it is that is necessary. It is very likely that your loved one who is facing the end of life is also worried about you. The dying can become focused on their caregivers as their world gets smaller and they are most concerned with what is right in front of them.

Just like in our everyday life, when you are with people, *be present* with them. Worry less about the busyness, and all the

121

things that need to be done. Offering love and comfort and even sitting in silence can bring reassurance and peace to the people who are dying.

For those of you giving care to a loved one who is chronically or terminally ill, I send you light now for clarity so that you will be reminded of the goodness you are doing.

Remember: To truly be present is worth everything. Plan on making mistakes in caregiving. Forgive yourself and learn. It is then you can move on and be present to honor the time left that you share.

Communicating at the End

It can be difficult for those at the end of life to focus and stay present for long conservations, therefore, we want to make sure the important parts of what we want them to know gets said while we have their attention. Of our senses, hearing is the last to fade as people are actively dying. This is important to note. A dying person can hear what you say to them even though they do not respond.

If you have a loved one dying right now, hold their hand, let them know you love them, tell them a few ways they have impacted your life, and that you won't forget them. They may also need to be forgiven or apologized to. This would be the time to do this. If you get a response verbally or nonverbally, this is a gift. If you do not, it is very likely they still heard you but are too weak to respond. I have told people, "It is okay not to respond. If you cannot, just know I love you." If you struggle to speak to them, the most important thing to convey is your love for the person. This is the greatest of gifts we can give to our dying loved one. In the end, love is the medicine that helps make dying tolerable. As one faces the end of their life, feeling that intense love is really all that matters. Another gift to give is the permission to go when they are ready. I have seen many hang on because they are taking care of those left behind. "It's ok to let go, I will be ok." These are important words to say. I wish you all meaningful conversations. "I love you" to the dying are three words that hold deep meaning. Love is the antidote to most of the things we suffer from.

The Dying Teach Us How to Live

Wisdom is often profound at the end of life. I was sitting and holding Abigail's hand as she was dying. Abigail said she had worried for years about this very moment. She shared that if we could live our lives backwards things would be clearer. She expressed being pleasantly surprised that this was calmer, and less scary than she had imagined. She was relieved that her pain was managed and that she didn't have the need to be in control any longer. Surrendering had become easier and she reflected, "I wish I had spent the time reassuring myself that I would be okay, regardless, instead of worrying. Worrying stole so many good days from me."

The lesson? Try hard to stay in the present moment and calm your fears by reassuring yourself. Worrying won't change the outcome but trusting and reassuring yourself certainly can. Be in the now.

A Comforted Heart

Love at The End of Life

In the same week, I had the privilege of being at the bedside of two patients whom I loved dearly. They were both young, courageous, and deeply loved. It was interesting to note that neither of them expressed fear at this phase in their lives. I'm confident it was because of the tremendous love they could feel from all the people gathered in their rooms.

The world gets smaller at the end of life. It is very focused and real, love and connection is what matters. My experience with these two young patients reminded me of the power of showing up for people. Genuinely loving someone can make a world of difference. Their legacies highlight what matters most, love. Tell someone today you love them. Love can heal, even if it can't cure.

Love Is What Matters

I facilitated a conference with a beautiful family deep in grief. The mother, who had terminal cancer, looked at all of her children and told them to be sure to go on living after she was gone and to love people, even though it's a risk because we can get hurt. "I will be comforted knowing you will love and be loved," she said. "It's worth it. Don't live life in fear. I know it hurts now because I'm dying, but look at all the joy our love brought. Nothing can take that from us." This was one of those unforgettable moments in my career.

A Comforted Heart

Today with all the stress, worry and anguish life can bring, it's important to stop, take a big breath, and remember who you love and who loves you. With this realization you can be comforted.

The Language of Dying

During a family conference to make end-of-life decisions about their mother, I noted the patient was in-and-out of our discussions. She was speaking in metaphors, which is very common in death and is a language we should all be paying attention to. People who are dying often try to communicate their shifting reality with such phrases as "I need to get home," "My train is leaving," "I have a boat waiting for me." These are not literal as we see it, but likely quite real for the dying person. I once had a patient who told me she had bought a train ticket for later that afternoon. It was then that I called her family to come to the hospice as she was giving me cues that her time was near. She died that afternoon, soon after her family arrived.

It is very important that you give your loved one permission to go. The dying will often wait for this from family/friends. It is best to ask questions such as "Where do you want to go? Describe it," instead of saying "Don't be silly. Remember, you are sick. "When I started working in End of Life Care twenty-five years ago, these conversations were considered to be hallucinations. We know now, this is the language of the dying.

Very often, my patients experience sightings of their deceased loved ones occur. How beautiful this is; there is protection from beyond. If you are caring for a dying loved one listen for metaphorical speech, rather than literal. Be creative in your listening. You can ask if they have seen any deceased loved ones. This may start a conversation with lots of information. "Mom, have you seen grandpa lately? How is he?"

We are not fluent in the "language of the dying," but we can learn a lot by listening with a different perspective and asking questions. The conversations are beautiful, and they make complete sense to the dying person. I will often say, "Safe travels as you leave and thank you for our time while you were here."

Love with Your Entire Heart

I will never forget a lovely 65-year-old woman who was very near death. She said her wish is that her death will teach others to live more intentionally. "Love with your entire heart and when it's your time to die, do not die with even one 'I love you' left unsaid." Simply profound.

Loving Yourself

I enjoy reminiscing at the end with people. Mike and I were speaking of all the work he and I had done in the last two years. I asked, "What do you feel is your greatest learning in our work together?" he proudly responded, "I found the person who deserves my love but wasn't getting it. It was me!"

We must love ourselves first, then love from there. Are you loving yourself enough? Or are you, like so many, full of criticism and self-doubt? Try looking at yourself as a small child. How would you speak to them? No doubt, you would offer understanding, tolerance, forgiveness and a deep abiding love. I'm so grateful for the lesson imparted by this patient and he asked me to share this simple wisdom with my world.

This Isn't the Life I Imagined

As I said goodbye to Ann we spoke candidly about what dying would be like. She said all of her end of life "duties" were complete, including graduation and wedding cards and a recording of her voice for her girls. Although her body had wasted away from illness, she mused "This wasn't the life I imagined, but I would do anything to keep it now."

This is one of the most profound lessons in gratitude I have ever been witness to. Ann had wanted more from her life prior to terminal cancer. In the end, she was thankful for what she had been given. Illness often brings perspective with it and perspective brings amazing healing opportunities

Signs of Loved Ones After Death

Being a grief therapist is often a peek into another world because I get to hear so many stories that confirm the continued bond of love. Love does not end at death. Most of us have lost someone we love to death, whether it be a grandparent, parent, child, partner, sibling, or friend.

Have you received any signs? Sometimes people look for a big sign, expecting grandiosity, and miss the simple. I'm going on record here to say I believe the deceased communicate often with us. Part of this belief is due to the hundreds of death vigils I have been part of where I have seen the dying communicate with their dead loved ones. I've studied after death communication with many spiritual and religious leaders which has allowed me to help others see that energy remains.

The grief sessions I do are filled with stories of visitations. Ask for a sign or visit and be open to the many beautiful ways the deceased can communicate. Customary to my conversations at the end, I will ask my patients how they will visit us from the "other side." One of my patients who died last year exclaimed, "As a butterfly!" Not too long after her death I found a completely intact monarch in the grill of my car. I remember it flying into the car as I was traveling at 70 MPH! I cherish her visit and I'm once again a believer.

Several years back, I was counseling a family after the sudden death of their son. They talked about always seeing dimes on the floor, on the ground, or on their desks. At first they thought nothing of this. After all who doesn't see money on the ground? Then as we continued to talk, they realized that many in the extended family were suddenly seeing dimes as well. It was when one of them found a dime in their bed after changing the sheets, that they started to wonder about this coincidence. They asked, "Why dimes?" I asked when their son had died. They answered, "October 10th" (10/10).

Look for the symbols representing your connection. If you feel you are being ignored because you haven't had a visit, I would encourage you to be more open and not expect a big experience.

A Comforted Heart

Dreams are visitations as well. Simple is beautiful. Be open and enjoy your meaningful visits. I believe the bond is forever. If inclined, feel free to keep a journal about these signs. They can later be affirmations for you if you are feeling alone or abandoned.

Often times beautiful surprises will be revealed that were once overshadowed by fear. Ask fear to step aside.

Kelly Grosklags

Chapter Eight
Allowing Yourself to Heal

Curing Versus Healing

There is a difference between healing and curing. My patients, of course, want their cancer cured. For some this will not ever be possible. For others, it may happen that they experience the joy of remission. In my practice, I talk about healing as a possibility for everyone, regardless of where they are in their journey.

Healing is the ability to face one's fears with courage, the possibility of forgiving someone, mending a relationship, forgiving and loving self, strengthening one's faith and learning to surrender. Some things cannot be cured or changed but we can experience healing by changing the way in which we see or think about things. Healing is always possible, and I have seen some of the most remarkable healing in the final days of a patient's life. Let yourself experience healing along your way.

Curing is on the physical level is not always possible. Healing focuses on the psychological, emotional and spiritual wounds. The gift of healing is a beautiful one.

A Comforted Heart

Lessons to Learn in Life

Everyone who comes into our life is a teacher or a mirror for what lessons we need to learn. Sometimes these learnings are painful. Often the painful lessons that break us open have the ability to heal us. It's important to learn the lessons and then move on. Going back to pain just because it's familiar does not mean you will learn the lesson deeper, it just means you will suffer more. Take from your teachers and release that which is not good for you. Learn, let go, and heal. The energy will be worth it.

Guilt Can Keep You Hostage

There is a part of life that keeps us hostage. That is Guilt. Over the years I have spent many sessions discussing this with patients who are living lives of constant regret and guilt which has completely robbed them of any joy or feeling of contentment. I see this so often embedded in grief. As one carries the burdens of "I didn't do enough," "I should have called her back last night," and "Why did I get upset with him?"

These statements won't bring back your beloved. Instead, the guilt and regret will only serve to keep you trapped in the darkest parts of your grief. Part of grieving is finding the new connection to those who are gone. We want our bonds with the deceased to feel healthy. Therefore, I encourage you to do your deep work around these issues. As you become less of a hostage to your guilt, your connection and bond to your deceased loved one will feel more pure and loving. This is when you realize "I can do this. This grief is not bigger than me."

"I Should Have..."

"I should have..." seems to be the topic of conversation when working with bereaved individuals. Many regret not doing or saying something to someone they loved before they died. This is a common theme in grief work and can derail us on our healing path.

If you are living with regret today, practice forgiveness beginning with self. Whatever it is that creates guilt for you, try to bring yourself back to that time and remind yourself of all the circumstances. People will hopefully realize they did the best they could. Dwelling on things that we cannot change only creates obstacles for our ability to move through and heal in our grief. What I encourage people to do to remedy the regret is to change their behavior in the present or the future. For instance, if you regret not expressing gratitude to somebody, be more grateful and expressive of this gratitude going forward. It can be very difficult to forgive one's self, when we are so entrenched in a guilt-ridden story. But exploring the many ways that self-forgiveness heals the soul is powerful and available to everyone.

Heavy Loads

Have you ever felt heavier after an experience with another person? Being attacked or judged by people in our lives is a very difficult thing to handle. My patients will be judged at times for making choices that center around taking care of themselves, whether it's saying no, or even yes to certain things. When I have felt attacked or judged, it's like someone dumped their baggage full of their own fear, jealousy, confusion, and/or anger onto me. It is not our job to carry around everybody's load in life so that they do not have to. If you're feeling pain, exhaustion, anxiety, depression, and/or fear, it is possible that you are carrying around the weight of others. Choose not to take the bags being handed to you.

A good visual and ritual in keeping good boundaries is to imagine literally giving back the suitcase to somebody who has dumped on you. See yourself giving them back this bag, as it is theirs to work through and heal. The only baggage that we have any business carrying around is our own. Only we can open our own suitcases in order to find those things that require our time for healing. It's time now to hand over the things that don't belong to you or serve your highest good. Lighter and healthier days are ahead as we surrender and release.

Celebrate Who You Are

Unfortunately, many people define themselves by their illnesses or disabilities. Because they are so engrossed in appointments or discussions about these issues, it dominates their time. People become disheartened when they define their totality based on their struggles.

Often, we judge ourselves harshly when looking at our external selves. My patients talk daily about not recognizing themselves any longer as disease has changed their appearance. Some diseases show on the outside more than others and people can become very self-conscious. It's important to remember you are first a human being who is dealing with an illness or disability.

Today, judge yourself on something kind that you have done for someone recently, or on the dedication and love you have shown to friends, family or self. When people change critical self- talk into loving talk, they look and feel better. It's important to acknowledge that you look different because of illness, *and* it's important to find your beauty that remains.

How you choose to view your life will make all the difference in how much you enjoy it. I've seen many courageous people in my years who do not allow the things that happen *to* them to *become* them. Celebrate all of who you are. You will find that if you change your outlook, your outlook changes.

Forgiveness Sets Us Free

The struggle to forgive is human. I do believe that illness, loss, or any life-change brings us the opportunity to evaluate our lives. We can assess what in our lives is causing us angst and work on releasing.

All of us have been hurt at some point in our lives. Hurt is unavoidable if we choose to enter into relationships. What we can hope for is the hurt that someone has caused us was not intentional, but if it was intentional you can still release the pain.

Holding onto anger is damaging to our health. I acknowledge it's difficult to forgive situations where there was not an apology. I also know there are situations that are unforgivable. Regardless, we all deserve to be free of that anger that is keeping the pain alive. We can release the angst by surrendering in prayer, meditation, exercise, writing letters, therapy, and detaching from the person if they remain in our life.

Forgiving someone does not mean that what they did to you was justifiable, nor does it offer excuses for poor behavior; the act of forgiveness just sets *you* free. It's difficult to let go sometimes, but I will say no one deserves to torment themselves. Ruminating can create such discord for us. My wish for you is when you think of the person or people who wronged you, you will eventually set them free from your mind and have the power to wish them light for their healing and move on. Forgiveness demands courage and is one of the finest ways to heal our spirits and be free.

Be Strong. Be Real.

It seems many people believe that the definition of strong is keeping our fears and insecurities to ourselves. Nothing could be further from the truth. It often takes uncomfortable feelings to motivate us to move in a different direction. When we share these fears with others, the discomfort can diminish and clarity will ensue. I feel quite fortunate that my work is real and I witness the strength and authenticity of the human spirit each day. An experience that has impacted my career is when I was able to be with a man who, for the first time in his life, cried from a place of deep pain. As he wept, he released wounds from far in the past that had been shoved down and hidden for years.

A Comforted Heart

Pain needs a way out the body; it's not meant to live there. I see people who attribute their physical and/or mental illness to traumas that have lived in their bodies for years. I believe there may something to this.

Showing our vulnerability allows for others to understand our wounds better and give us support. This enables our energy to go into cathartic release rather than into being spent suppressing the pain. Often, there is nothing to "fix." It is the release that heals.

I see the strong as those who have the courage to be real. For me, I appreciate *real* in my relationships. Real is what heals us. Be vulnerable today. Be strong. Be real. If you show *your* vulnerabilities, you are allowing others to show theirs, too. This is what strengthens our connections.

You Are Courageous

It's interesting how people often say, "I'm not courageous. Inside I'm shaking and scared like crazy." Being fearless and courageous are not one and the same. In fact, my most courageous patients are the ones who, despite their fear, still get up each day and face what it has in store for them.

You are courageous. Be proud when you are willing to face something or try something despite the trepidation around it. Let fear fuel your courage rather than hinder it. After you face something that is filled with fear, tell your mind and body, "Thank you courageous ones!"

A Comforted Heart

Inside of You Are the Answers

Daily I see people struggle to find answers to difficult questions. They often look to me for help. Sometimes we just have to sit with the questions and if we become very quiet, we can hear more. Inside of you are the answers. Your answers.

Intuition, we all have it, although it's more developed and understood in some people than in others. There are many overwhelming questions to ask and decisions to be made along this journey we are on. Your inner knowing will guide you if you learn to become fluent in it. But first, you must be still in order to hear. As it is said, "The quieter we become, the more we hear." If you are facing something that is overwhelming, take a breath, get your feet grounded and listen. You will hear what you need.

Vulnerability Is Strength

I see variations of strength every day. I admire those who can show what they feel. People who cry in response to their sadness are strong and authentic. We, as humans, are born with the ability to cope and be resilient. Sometimes we need to change our messages to ourselves and remember that being vulnerable is not a sign of weakness. Rather, it is a sign of courage.

Give thought today to the messages you grew up with concerning vulnerability. If these messages are shaming and negative, I encourage you to work on releasing them. Invite in gentle and authentic messages to match the feelings you're having. Those who will be vulnerable are some of the wisest and strongest people I know. I admire the ability to be real and show fear. Being real is the way we can be more present in our lives. I wish you the ability to always be present in all the experiences of your lifetime.

I Wish for You a Comforted Heart

My hope is that the time spent within these pages has provided you with fresh insights, a renewed sense of hope and a lighter spirit. While writing, I was often reminded of several values that have become the cornerstones of how I aspire to live my life. My beautiful patients let me into their healing journeys and graciously show me what truly matters in life. For me, it comes down to being loved. Love is the antidote for much of our suffering and has the power to heal, even when cure is not possible.

Gratitude, perspective, forgiveness and surrender are lessons I'm taught each day in my sessions. It is because of what I learn daily in my work that I strive to be better, braver, express love deeply, trust more and be as authentic as I can. It has been my truest privilege to be let into the lives of countless people over the years and be witness to vulnerability, resiliency and healing. It is my hope as you took your own individual path through this book that you felt a sense of belonging and hopefully less isolated. I hope you will return to it as often as you need. Remember to be present to this moment and as always, I wish you for you **A Comforted Heart**.

The design you see here is the Mandala. It is a beautiful healing symbol.

The Mandala is an ancient Sanskrit word meaning "completion, wholeness, and circle." Many spiritual traditions use the Mandala in their teachings and rituals as a focal point for meditation; to move from the outer world into the inner. Mandalas can be recognized in the natural world in the form of the sun, the earth, a flower, or any concentric pattern displayed; so it follows that we can also see the Mandala as a mystical representation of our underlying unity in this world that we all share. As a gateway between the spiritual realm and our earthly existence, the Mandala, as a contemplative tool, has amazing potential to help us hear our intuitive promptings and to gain clarity. This symbol can restore a feeling of peace and calm while imparting an innate understanding of the mysteries of the universe. I feel immense gratitude to have discovered the beauty and mystery of Mandalas and to be part of The Great Mandala, the Great Circle of Life.

Barbara Fleetham

A Comforted Heart

Quick Reference Guide

A Comforted Heart

About the Author

Kelly Grosklags, LICSW, BCD, Fellow, American Academy of Grief Counseling

For nearly 25 years Kelly has dedicated her practice to minimizing suffering through her work in oncology, palliative care and hospice. An experienced therapist and gifted speaker, Kelly created *Conversations with Kelly* as a public healing forum to broaden her reach as a psychotherapist, social worker and healer for patients and families.

Kelly frequently speaks about end-of-life care, and grief and loss issues at hospitals, clinical conferences, churches, funeral homes and schools. Her passionate and supportive demeanor helps patients, caregivers and health professionals connect with the wisdom of dying a good death, making life more meaningful, coping with depression and anxiety, transforming fear into hope and healing versus curing.

Kelly is a Board Certified Diplomate in clinical social work and earned a fellowship in grief counseling from the American Academy of Health Care Professionals. She earned a Master's Degree in clinical social work from the University of St. Thomas/University of St. Catherine. She is a proud former board member of Angel Foundation, a non-profit organization based in Minnesota that supports families living with cancer.

She is the author of *A Comforted Heart*, published in 2017. Her private psychotherapy practice is located in Minneapolis, Minnesota.

40606263R00084

Made in the USA
Middletown, DE
30 March 2019